SERIES EDITOR: LEE JOHN

OSPREY MILITARY WARRIO

IMPERIAL GUARDSMAN
1799-1815

TEXT BY
PHILIP J. HAYTHORNTHWAITE

COLOUR PLATES BY
RICHARD HOOK

First published in Great Britain in 1997 by OSPREY, a division of Reed Books, Michelin House, 81 Fulham Road, London SW3 6RB, Auckland and Melbourne

ISBN 1 85532 662 0

Military Editor: Iain MacGregor
Design: Alan Hamp @ Design for Books

Filmset in Singapore by Pica Ltd.
Printed through World Print Ltd., Hong Kong

For a catalogue of all books published by Osprey Military please write to:
Osprey Marketing, Reed Books, Michelin House, 81 Fulham Road, London SW3 6RB

Publisher's note

Readers may wish to study this title in conjunction with the following Osprey publications:

MAA 257 *Napoleon's Campaigns in Italy*
MAA 79 *Napoleon's Eygptian Campaign*
MAA 87 *Napoleon's Marshals*
MAA 64 *Napoleon's Cuirassiers & Carabiniers*
MAA 55 *Napoleon's Dragoons & Lancers*
MAA 68 *Napoleon's Line Chasseurs*
MAA 76 *Napoleon's Hussars*
MAA 83 *Napoleon's Guard Cavalry*
MAA 141 *Napoleon's Line Infantry*
MAA 146 *Napoleon's Light Infantry*
MAA 153 *Napoleon's Guard Infantry (1)*
MAA 160 *Napoleon's Guard Infantry (2)*
MAA 199 *Napoleon's Specialist Troops*
MAA 88 *Napoleon's Italian & Neoplitan Troops*
MAA 44 *Napoleon's German Allies (1) Westfalia & Kleve-Berg*
MAA 43 *Napoleon's German Allies (2) Nassau & Oldenberg*
MAA 90 *Napoleon's German Allies (3) Saxony*
MAA 106 *Napoleon's German Allies (4) Bavaria*
MAA 122 *Napoleon's German Allies (5) Hessen-Darmstadt & Hessen-Kassel*
MAA 211 *Napoleon's Overseas Army*
MAA 227 *Napoleon's Sea Soldiers*
MAA 77 *Flags of the Napoleonic Wars (1)*
MAA 78 *Flags of the Napoleonic Wars (2)*
MAA 115 *Flags of the Napoleonic Wars (3)*
CAM 2 *Austerlitz 1805*
CAM 33 *Aspern & Wagram 1809*
CAM 48 *Salamanca 1809*
CAM 25 *Leipzig 1813*
CAM 15 *Waterloo 1815*

Artist's Note

IMPERIAL GUARDSMAN 1799-1815

INTRODUCTION

Napoleon's Imperial Guard was one of the most famous military formations in history, and quite distinct from the guard corps of other European sovereigns of the period. The Imperial Guard could perform ceremonial duties as well as any, but it was primarily an élite combat formation of the army. By supplying personnel to other units, it provided a training school for the remainder of the army, and although it expanded to represent a considerable portion of France's military establishment, it remained Napoleon's personal guard and was accorded care and attention which set its members above the rest of the army. However, the Guard's privileged status provided little shield against the rigours of campaign and the brutal nature of combat during the Napoleonic Wars.

In the following sections, most attention is given to those aspects of the Imperial Guard and its service which were different from the conditions experienced by the remainder of the French army.

Napoleon wearing his most familiar uniform, that of the *Chasseurs à Cheval* of the Imperial Guard. The breast-star and the first of the medals are those of the *Légion d'Honneur*; the second medal is that of the Order of the Iron Crown. (Print after Horace Vernet)

REGIMENTS AND RECRUITS

The Imperial Guard was so large and complex an organisation that conditions of entry and service varied considerably. It is therefore necessary to consider the principal Guard formations and their source of recruits. The posting of a soldier to one or other Guard unit was not necessarily permanent; there was considerable interchange between regiments, especially in the case of officers and NCOs, who are covered in a separate section.

The creation of the Consular Guard (*Garde des Consuls*) as an élite veteran bodyguard for the French head of state dated from the end of 1799; the *Chasseurs* and *Grenadiers à Pied* took 2 December 1799 as their date of creation, although the decree specifying their organisation was issued only on 3 January 1800. From the very beginning, Napoleon personally superintended the entry of personnel and promotion of NCOs and officers; he set the original conditions of admission to the Guard. At the outset he declared that the Consular Guard should be "a model for the army" and established strict entrance criteria: Guardsmen should have participated in three campaigns; have been wounded or given proof of their bravery; they should be patriotic and of good conduct; not less than 25 years of age and at least 1.78m tall; and they should be literate. (Some confusion may arise over the height qualification when expressed in feet: the contemporary French foot measured 12.8 English inches.) Thus entrants to the Guard transferred from the line were all experienced campaigners with a good record even before they received what came to be regarded as the ultimate accolade, entry into Napoleon's personal bodyguard.

From the beginning, however, exceptions were made to the entry conditions. Literacy was demanded only of NCOs, and while the height qualification varied (chasseurs were accepted shorter than grenadiers), the well known example of Jean-Roch Coignet shows how a distinguished soldier might evade the restrictions. A member of the 96th *Demi-Brigade*, Coignet was an ideal candidate for the guard in all respects except his height: but Capt. Renard of the *Grenadiers à Pied*, anxious to secure such a valiant man for his own company, conspired with General Davout himself (commander of the corps of grenadiers) to have Coignet evade the height restriction. At Davout's suggestion he put two packs of playing cards under each foot, inside his stockings, to ensure he met the minimum requirement.

Napoleon, in the uniform of First Consul, with the staff of the Consular Guard; at the right is his Mameluke servant, Roustam. (Engraving by C. Turner after Masquerier)

Stringent conditions for recruits to the Old Guard infantry (the senior regiments) were maintained even when the line was being filled by under-age conscripts. In March 1813 Napoleon decreed that 12 years' service and several campaigns were necessary for the admittance of an officer or NCO, ten years' service for lower ranks, and candidates without such qualifications had to be approved by Napoleon in person. In April 1806 2nd Regiments of chasseurs and grenadiers were created, but they were amalgamated in 1809 to economise on the huge expense of maintaining the Guard. New 2nd Regiments were formed in May 1811, with only eight years' service required for entry. A Guard Veteran Company was formed in July 1801 from men with at least three years' service who were no longer fit for active duty; another was formed in 1807 and an artillery company was formed in January 1812. They performed routine guard and security duties, including duties at the imperial palaces.

Napoleon in the uniform of the *Grenadiers à Pied* of the Imperial Guard. (Print after Delarouche)

Similar qualifications to those of the infantry applied to the senior units of Guard cavalry, the *Grenadiers à Cheval* and *Chasseurs à Cheval* . The former, like *Grenadiers à Pied*, selected the taller recruits (their size magnified by their bearskin caps, and their aloof demeanour contributed to their nickname 'Gods' – or, from their boots, 'big heels'). The *Chasseurs à Cheval*, deriving from the earlier corps of Bonaparte's Guides (and colloquially retaining the latter name, especially for imperial escort-duty), were the finest light cavalry and usually provided Napoleon's personal escort. The loyalty they showed towards Napoleon was reciprocated by the fact they he most often wore their uniform.

The Guard artillery also dated from the period of the Consular Guard, initially a company of *Artillerie Légère* with eight guns, with an artillery train added in 1800. Although enlarged in 1802/3, it was not until 1806 that it was formed into a regiment of horse artillery (*Artillerie à Cheval*).

The next unit added to the Guard was its most exotic, and its first foreign element: Mamelukes who had allied themselves to the French army during the Egyptian expedition and who had accompanied the army on its return to France, bringing their dependants. They were organised into a squadron for the Consular Guard, and although trained in ordinary tactics, they retained their traditional élan, oriental costume and weaponry. Their integration was not without problems: shortly after his arrival in France, Captain Ibrahim Bey shot dead two members of a crowd who were jeering at him for his

Officer of Mamelukes of the Imperial Guard, a painting by Eugène Lami which exemplifies the exotic nature of the costume and equipment, and their intimidating appearance. (The Royal Collection © Her Majesty The Queen)

unusual appearance. His plea that he had only acted as he would have done in Egypt prevented serious punishment, but he was retired to Marseilles on a pension and forbidden to carry arms. Napoleon insisted that the Mameluke squadron should cost no more than a similar unit of chasseurs, so they received reduced pay to defray the additional expenses of their costume and equipment; however, they had to be allocated more funds. (The oriental costume was impressive and probably intimidating to their enemies, but not entirely practical: Ibrahim Bey, who finally returned to active service in 1814, was wounded and captured when his turban came untied and fell over his eyes). As a unique concession, the Mamelukes' dependants were also given pay, with male children joining the unit when they reached the age of 16. As it was impossible to continue to recruit genuine Mamelukes, Frenchmen and other foreigners from as far afield as the Ionian Islands and North Africa were later admitted.

The next unit to form part of the Guard was a squadron of *gendarmes,* who were assembled for service in Paris in July 1801. Taken into the Consular Guard in March 1802, they provided security for government buildings and later performed similar duties in the field. This *Gendarmerie d'Elite* originally included both mounted and dismounted companies, but the latter were discontinued. Their members were selected carefully – initially they had to be army NCOs who had transferred to the *Gendarmerie,* aged 25-45 years and with service in four campaigns. Later recruits came from the ordinary *Gendarmerie* or were

Marshal Jean Baptiste Bessières, Duke of Istria (1767-1813), Colonel-General of the Guard cavalry. (Engraving by C. State after Hédouin)

selected from drafts of conscripts. On campaign they protected the imperial headquarters and Napoleon's person, secured lines of communication and were equally adept when acting as conventional heavy cavalry; at home they assisted the ordinary *Gendarmerie* in the apprehension of *réfractaires* – those endeavouring to escape conscription.

On 17 September 1803 Napoleon decreed the formation of a battalion of seamen for the Consular Guard, initially to man the boats transporting the staff on the invasion of England. The unit's title, *Marins de la Garde*, should be translated as 'seamen', not 'marines' (for which the French is *Infanterie de la Marine*) and it was as seamen that they were recruited. Each maritime prefect was required to supply a draft of recruits, men of proven record and physical ability, and many came from the south of France and Corsica. They received the same pay as the Guard cavalry but maintained a maritime character: their ranks included the naval terms *capitaine de vaisseau* (battalion commander – equating to the captain of a ship of the line), *capitaine de frégate* (naval commander), *enseigne* (lieutenant) and *maître* (sergeant), while companies were styled *équipages* ('crews') instead of companies. The corps fluctuated in size, and a small detachment accompanied Napoleon to Elba. Trained as infantry, they were equally adept at manning small boats and serving as engineers, and in Moscow in 1812 two companies were equipped with six 12-pdr. guns and two howitzers. Napoleon's comment on this most versatile part of his Guard was appropriate: "They have been none the less good seamen, because they have shown themselves the best of soldiers. When required, we have found them seamen, soldiers, artillerymen, engineers, everything!"

The year 1804 saw the formation of the *vélite* organisation – covered below in the section on officers and NCOs – and also the proclamation of the Empire, whereupon (from 10 May 1804) the Consular Guard was re-titled the Imperial Guard (*La Garde Impériale*).

In April 1806 another Guard regiment was formed, the dragoons, and in 1807 they were retitled the 'Empress's Dragoons' (*Dragons de L'Impératrice*). Each line dragoon regiment supplied a dozen of their best men to form the first two squadrons; the third squadron was composed of *vélites*, and other Guard units also supplied recruits. A further draft of line dragoons was taken in the following year. Also in April 1806 a unit of *Ouvriers d'Administration* was formed to oversee the Guard's transport, supply wagons and ambulances.

In September 1806 Napoleon decreed the formation of a small corps of *Gendarmes d'Ordonnance*, using the ancient title of the royal bodyguard

TOP LEFT **Marshal Edouard Adolphe Casimir Joseph Mortier, Duke of Treviso (1768-1835), Colonel-General of the Artillery and Seamen of the Imperial Guard. (Engraving by Lacoste after Demoraine)**

TOP RIGHT **The two styles of uniform worn by the *Chasseurs à Cheval* of the Guard: left, coat with aiguillette, worn with a braided waistcoat; right, hussar uniform. (Print by Montigneul after Eugène Lami)**

of King Henri IV. In an attempt to associate the old nobility with the new Empire, Napoleon called for volunteers aged 18-40 years who had a private income of at least 600 francs per annum, and who could supply their own horses and travel at their own expense to Mayence (Mainz), where the corps was to be organised. Five mounted companies were formed, some of which saw active service, but the unit did not fit easily into the Guard (the men each provided their own servant, for example, to act as groom and batman). The ordinary guardsmen were suspicious of such privileged status, and as they were not especially suited for hard campaigning, the unit was disbanded in October 1807. Some members were commissioned or retained as *vélites* and others were discharged.

Also in 1806 Napoleon began the enlargement of the Guard infantry. The existing regiments were still recruited from the line, from men of good record, aged under 35, with ten years' service and the height requirement of 1.78m for grenadiers and artillery and 1.72m for chasseurs.

It proved difficult to provide enough recruits, however, even after reducing the qualification of service to six years and dispensing with the height restriction for holders of the *Légion d'Honneur*. A further consideration was the great expense: the Guards' pay and conditions cost much more per capita than line troops. The solution was the creation of junior Guard regiments affiliated to and administered by the existing corps of grenadiers and chasseurs. In October 1806 a regiment of *Fusiliers-Chasseurs* was formed, with recruits that came from the *vélites*, from selected conscripts from the line and from departmental reserve companies, with a cadre of officers and NCOs from the existing Guard. A regiment of *Fusiliers-Grenadiers*, administered by the grenadier corps, was authorised in December 1806. In 1809 these new units were styled

'Young Guard' to differentiate them from the original 'Old Guard'.

In March 1807 the first wholly foreign regiment was created, the Polish *Chevau-Légers* (light horse), recruited from volunteers who were landowners, or their sons. They had to be aged 18-45, able to furnish their own equipment and horse, and be expert horsemen. The regiment's reputation was made by their charge on the Spanish position at Somosierra (30 November 1808), and in 1809 they were armed with lances and became the Guard's 1st Regiment of *Chevau-Légers-Lanciers*. A 3rd Regiment of Guard lancers was also Polish (actually composed mostly of Lithuanian nobility). It was formed in July 1812 but was almost annihilated in the Russian campaign. It was incorporated in the 1st Regiment in March 1813. The Polish corps was disbanded in 1814, save for a squadron which followed Napoleon to Elba and which in 1815 formed part of the Guard lancer regiment.

In 1808 the Guard artillery was augmented by the formation of a corps of foot artillery. Enlarged progressively by the formation from 1809 of Young Guard companies, the Guard artillery became a very powerful force. Its strength had increased to 96 guns by May 1811 (24 with the horse artillery) and to 196 by April 1813 (36 with horse artillery).

Between January and April 1809 eight new Young Guard regiments were formed, affiliated – as before – to the corps of grenadiers and chasseurs. Although they enjoyed the prestige and privileges of Guard status, they were paid as line troops as an economy measure. The rank and file were selected from the best men of each successive class of con-scripts, while officers and NCOs came in part from existing Guard regiments (part of the continual process of transfer of per-sonnel within the Guard as experienced men were promoted from a senior unit into a junior). Four regiments were styled *tirailleurs* (literally 'skir-mishers', though the title was selected for reasons of morale rather than to imply a tactical function), two

One of the most famous images of the Imperial Guard: Théodore Géricault's spectacular picture of an officer of the *Chasseurs à Cheval*, exhibited in 1812, which depicts full dress uniform, including panther-skin saddle-cover, and exemplifies the élan traditionally associated with the light cavalry. (Print after Géricault)

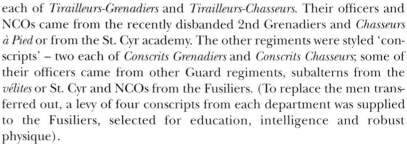

each of *Tirailleurs-Grenadiers* and *Tirailleurs-Chasseurs*. Their officers and NCOs came from the recently disbanded 2nd Grenadiers and *Chasseurs à Pied* or from the St. Cyr academy. The other regiments were styled 'conscripts' – two each of *Conscrits Grenadiers* and *Conscrits Chasseurs*; some of their officers came from other Guard regiments, subalterns from the *vélites* or St. Cyr and NCOs from the Fusiliers. (To replace the men transferred out, a levy of four conscripts from each department was supplied to the Fusiliers, selected for education, intelligence and robust physique).

For the men promoted into a junior regiment it was important to retain their superior pay and status. Conversely, it was intended that the junior regiments be used as a source of recruits for the senior; after two years' service in the *Tirailleurs* men might be admitted to the Fusiliers, and after four more years to the Old Guard.

The title 'conscript' was not popular, and after the renaming of the *Tirailleurs-Grenadiers* and *Tirailleurs-Chasseurs* as *Tirailleurs* and *Voltigeurs* respectively, in December 1810, the following February the *Conscrits-Grenadiers* became the 3rd and 4th *Tirailleurs* and the *Conscrits-Chasseurs* became the 3rd and 4th *Voltigeurs*. From May 1811 these two categories were expanded, mostly in 1813/14, until there were 19 regiments of each in addition to a number of 'duplicated' (*bis*) regiments which existed in 1813. In addition to serving as combatant units, Napoleon intended that they serve as a training ground for NCOs of the line, with *tirailleurs* as corporals and fusiliers as sergeants. To this end an Instructional Battalion of the Guard was formed at Fontainebleau, where selected personnel could be trained.

To express his satisfaction with the mobilised 'cohorts' of the National Guard in the northern departments, and to persuade National Guardsmen to remain with their colours, in January 1810 Napoleon decreed the formation of a regiment of *Gardes Nationales de la Garde*. The men were taken from existing National Guard units and field officers from the line; some deserted and were replaced by conscripts. In 1813 the regiment became the 7th *Voltigeurs*.

In July 1810 Napoleon created a company of engineers (*Sapeurs du Génie*), originally as fire-fighters for the imperial palaces and to accompany headquarters on campaign. They ranked as members of the Old Guard, and the unit was later increased to battalion strength by the formation of Young Guard companies.

The incorporation of the Kingdom of Holland into France included the merger of that state's military forces with the French army. In September 1810 a 2nd Regiment of *Grenadiers à Pied* was created for the Imperial Guard, from the Royal Guard of the Kingdom of Holland; when the 2nd (French) regiment of grenadiers was re-constituted in May 1811, the 'Dutch' regiment was numbered the 3rd. It included a veteran company at Amsterdam. The regiment was destroyed in the 1812 Russian campaign and was disbanded officially in February 1813. The same source also provided one of the Imperial Guard's best known cavalry regiments, when the Dutch Guard Hussars, augmented by men from other Dutch cavalry regiments, became the 2nd *Chevau-Légers-Lanciers* of the Guard, otherwise known (from the striking colour of their uniforms) as the Red Lancers (*Lanciers Rouges*). Subsequently it accepted French recruits, and in February 1813 the cavalry of the *Garde de Paris* was incorporated.

The third Guard unit which originated in Holland was a corps of cadets whose fathers had been killed in action; Napoleon used them as the basis for a cadet corps in which French orphans were to be educated and trained as the Guardsmen of the future. The two Dutch battalions were put in the care of the Dutch grenadiers in February 1811, and in the following month were instituted officially as the *Pupilles* of the Guard. The organisation was enlarged to nine battalions until it represented about one-sixth of the Guard – the largest unit but with the lowest pay and privileges. Its members came from all parts of the empire, and it's officers and NCO instructors came from existing Guard units. In 1813/1́4 the *Pupilles* provided recruits for the Young Guard and the 7th *Tirailleurs* was formed from them, and in 1814 the battalion stationed at Versailles helped defend Paris with great determination.

Left: trumpeter of the *Chasseurs à Cheval* of the Guard; right: officer with standard, Mamelukes. (Print by Lacoste after Guerin)

The enlargement of the Guard and the resulting need for more transport led in 1811 to a company of the *Ouvriers* forming the basis of a Guard *Train des Equipages* to supervise Guard vehicles. In September 1811 a light infantry corps of *Flanqueurs-Chasseurs* was created, recruited from the sons or nephews of rangers of the imperial or public forests. They had to be at least 18 years old and their background was meant to produce men already skilled in woodcraft and skirmishing. It was intended that after five years' service they should succeed to their fathers' or uncles' posts, but after the losses in Russia in 1812 the unit was re-formed by ordinary recruits, as was the equivalent unit of *Flanqueurs-Grenadiers* created in March 1813.

The enlargement of the Guard increased the interchange of personnel. The senior units continued to provide officers and NCOs for the junior, and as status within the Guard was not dependent exclusively upon the unit in which an individual was serving, the accounting system was complicated. By 1812 it had become necessary to define membership of the Old, Middle and Young Guards.

Old Guard

1st Grenadiers and *Chasseurs à Pied*, Grenadiers and *Chasseurs à Cheval*, Dragoons, *1st Chevau-Légers-Lanciers*, Mamelukes, *Gendarmerie d'Elite*, Seamen, *Sapeurs*, Veterans, Old Guard Artillery; officers and NCOs of 2nd Grenadiers and *Chasseurs à Pied*, Fusiliers and Young Guard Artillery; officers of 2nd *Chevau-Légers-Lanciers*, 3rd Grenadiers, *Train d'Artillerie*, field officers and captains of *Voltigeurs*, *Tirailleurs*, *Flanqueurs* and *Gardes Nationales*.

LEFT **Eugène de Beauharnais (1781-1824), Napoleon's stepson and viceroy of Italy, in the uniform of the *Chasseurs à Cheval* of the Guard. (Engraving by C. A. Powell after H. Scheffer)**

Cavalry of the Guard: left, an officer of the 1st (Polish) *Chevau-Légers-Lanciers*; right, a trooper of the dragoons, with the waist-belt worn over the shoulder. (Print by Lacoste after Eugène Lami)

Middle Guard

NCOs and men of 3rd Grenadiers (including their Veteran company), 2nd *Chevau-Légers-Lanciers*, *Train d'Artillerie*, *Italian Vélites*, *Ouvriers*; rank and file (including corporals) of 2nd Grenadiers and *Chasseurs à Pied*, Fusiliers.

Young Guard

Train des Equipages, *Pupilles*; subalterns and men of *Voltigeurs*, *Tirailleurs*, *Flanqueurs*, *Gardes Nationales*; NCOs and men of Young Guard Artillery.

In 1812 a squadron of Lithuanian Tartars was attached to the Polish lancers. They were expert light horsemen who retained their traditional costume. To replenish the Guard after the disaster in Russia in 1812, Napoleon drew heavily upon the line regiments, including units serving in Spain (the 14th and 15th *Tirailleurs* and *Voltigeurs* were recruited from Joseph Bonaparte's old Spanish Royal Guard). In 1813 he augmented the cavalry not by the formation of new regiments but by the addition of Young Guard squadrons to existing units: *Chasseurs à Cheval*, both *Chevau-Léger-Lancier* regiments, dragoons and *Grenadiers à Cheval*. Although these were members of the Guard, they received only line pay and had some uniform distinctions. They did not wear the aiguillettes of the Old Guard, and the Young Guard squadrons of the 2nd *Chevau-Légers-Lanciers* wore blue jackets instead of the regimental red.

In addition, some new cavalry regiments were raised. In April 1813 the 1st-4th *Gardes d'Honneur* were created, recruited from the nobility and other prominent families, all ostensibly volunteers, who provided their own mounts and equipment, with the wealthier families finding the funds to equip the less affluent. They had instructors from the Old Guard and in time became proficient. However, some non-French members deserted, and there was a suspicion that the creation of the *Gardes d'Honneur* was as much a political act as a military one, and an attempt to bind the leading families more closely to Napoleon's regime.

The last category of units formed for the Guard were the light cavalry scouts or *Eclaireurs*, created in December 1813 – the 1st Regt. *Eclaireurs-Grenadiers*, the 2nd Dragoons and the 3rd Lancers. Many were selected conscripts, but some experienced men included the transfer of *Gardes d'Honneur* into the grenadiers and the surviving Lithuanian Tartars into the lancers, with Guard or line officers and NCOs.

There were two other foreign units: the *Lanciers de Berg*, which ranked as part of the Guard from December 1809, and the ephemeral Polish battalion, formed in October 1813 from Polish units of the *Grande Armée* and the Vistula Legion. The Polish battalion was granted the pay and privileges of the 2nd Grenadiers but suffered heavily and was disbanded in December 1813.

Whatever the merits of using the Guard as a

training ground for officers and NCOs of the line, it also damaged the line units. The selection of the best conscripts deprived the line of much of its most promising material. Men who had distinguished themselves, whose presence would have enhanced line units, could hardly be refused the honour of entry to the Guard; a characteristic example was the renowned sergeant-major Guindey of the 10th Hussars, who in a sabre fight had killed Prince Louis Ferdinand of Prussia at Saalfeld in 1806. This intrepid man became an assistant-adjutant-major in the *Grenadiers à Cheval*, and was killed in a charge against Bavarian cavalry at Hanau.

Officers and NCOs

In addition to the interchange of personnel between units, the transfer of men from senior corps to be NCOs in the junior left room for promotions within regiments of men from the ranks. Literacy was a qualification for NCO status, though a deserving man might evade this stipulation: Coignet was promoted to corporal in the grenadiers while illiterate, and was taught to read and write by his squad while he instructed them in practical soldiering. NCOs could also be commissioned as officers, an event sometimes commemorated by the ceremony of the ex-NCO's company shooting his pack to pieces, as a symbol of his new status.

The Guard *vélite* organisation was created by Napoleon in 1804 as a training school of potential officers and NCOs. Its title was borrowed from the early Roman military, in which *vélite* (from the Latin *veles*) described a young skirmisher not sufficiently mature to be a legionary. It

RIGHT **'Eagle'-bearer of the** *Grenadiers à Pied* **of the Imperial Guard. The 'Eagle', the gilded-bronze statuette on top of the colour-pole, represented the mutual bond which existed between Napoleon and his troops, and was a regiment's most precious possession. (Print after Charlet)**

BELOW, LEFT **Lithuanian Tartar of the Imperial Guard, illustrating the vaguely Cossack-style uniform of that corps.**

BELOW, RIGHT **Officer of the** *Gardes d'Honneur* **of the Imperial Guard. (Print after 'Job')**

also prevented causing offence to republicans by avoiding the term 'cadet', which had aristocratic connotations. Provision was made for the numbers of the Guard *vélite* to be made up be conscripts, but in the event, enough young men volunteered since it offered the opportunity to learn the military trade as a privileged member of the rank and file, before passing to a line regiment as an officer.

A battalion of *vélites* was formed for each existing branch of the Guard infantry, styled *Vélite-Grenadiers* or *Vélite-Chasseurs*; officers and NCOs were taken from the Guard. *Vélites* received Guard pay, but their parents had to pay 200 francs per annum into the regimental fund (300 for *vélites* in the cavalry and artillery; the former had a squadron of *vélites* for each regiment). Recruits had to be of respectable family, aged at least 20 (though in the event of insufficient volunteers, those aged 18 might be accepted), and of some education. Being directed towards the more affluent members of society, it was also an attempt by Napoleon to gain support from the most important families.

For training the *vélites* served in their own units, but on campaign they were distributed among the parent regiments. From 1807 (1811 for the cavalry) they were totally absorbed. In 1809, however, two Italian *vélite* battalions were raised as bodyguards. They were for Elisa Bonaparte, the Grand Duchess of Tuscany, in Florence, and for Napoleon's brother-in-law, Prince Borghese, in Turin. As usual the stipulation was 200 francs per annum, from young men of good family, with officers and NCOs from the Guard.

The *vélite* organisation was popular among the sons of the upper classes; education as an officer at the school at Fontainebleau was more expensive, at 1,200 francs per annum (though less arduous and with higher certainty of gaining a commission). *Vélites* avoided conscription into a unit not of their choosing and, as Elzéar Blaze recalled, it enabled them to wear the uniform of an élite unit without waiting for training to be completed.

Their incorporation into the Guard was not without friction. Jean-Baptiste Barrès, who joined the chasseurs as a *vélite* for the 1805 campaign, remarked that the young men looked like girls beside the moustached veterans. The latter resented the intrusion of inexperienced youths

Drum-major of the *Grenadiers à Pied* of the Guard. This office was held most famously by one of the Guard's best-known members, Jean Nicolas Sénot (1761-1837), who had served in the army of the *ancien régime* from the age of eleven. (Print after Raffet)

into the Guard; but their attitude changed when it was realised that as members of affluent families, most *vélites* had money with which to treat the ordinary Guardsmen. Even after campaign service, promotion from the *vélites* was not automatic. Barrès noted that favouritism was a factor, and in his own case promotion was delayed by the hatred of his sergeant-major, who resented Barrès' laughter when he (the sergeant-major) was wounded at Eylau.

Officers' promotion could also be slow, unless they were prepared to transfer to units of lesser prestige. General Dorsenne suggested that Guard officers should be drawn from the better families, but Napoleon remarked that he preferred old soldiers of humble background, without private resources, who were more loyal because they were dependent upon him. Officers' promotion in the Guard was slower in wartime than in peace, as distinguished line officers could hardly be refused the reward of transfer to the Guard, instead of vacancies being filled from within the Guard. Influence with those in authority was also a factor, as Lieutenant Charles Parquin of the 13th *Chasseurs à Cheval* discovered: on leave in Paris, he encountered General Lefebvre-Desnoëttes, colonel of the Guard *Chasseurs à Cheval,* and asked to join the Guard, and as Marshal Marmont was passing, cited the latter as a referee of his previous conduct. Nine days later Parquin was on parade as an officer of the Guard.

The high command of the Guard was unusual in possessing four 'colonel-generals': Marshals Davout (who commanded the corps of grenadiers), Soult (the chasseurs), Bessières (the cavalry) and Mortier (artillery and seamen). These waited on Napoleon in weekly rotation, were responsible only to him, and commanded the Guard at reviews. However, most led their own corps on campaign, with Bessières often commanding the Guard cavalry and Marshal Lefebvre the infantry. Quite deliberately, the Guard never had a single commander save Napoleon himself, for reasons of his own security. As he wrote to his brother Joseph on 31 May 1806, advising on the establishment of his own guard as king of Naples, "Do not organise your guard so as to be under the control of a single commander; nothing can be more dangerous."

EVERYDAY LIFE

Although it did not so much affect the units formed by the massive enlargement of the Young Guard, for the remainder, membership of the Imperial Guard brought with it great privileges. As Blaze admitted, Guardsmen were "little Sardanapaluses" compared with the troops of the line. The superior status of the Guard was unquestioned; indeed, whenever a Guard unit encountered one of the line on the march, the latter had to halt, present arms, lower its colours and sound a salute, which the Guard would acknowledge without halting. Similarly, when Napoleon was with the army, the Guard would turn out its guard posts under arms, with trumpets and drumbeats, only for him. Other generals received only a turn-out, without arms or music.

The difference in status affected all ranks, with each Guardsman being equivalent to the next rank up in the line: a Guard private equated with a line corporal, a Guard lieutenant with a line captain, and so on. Blaze recalled how his regiment once deliberately held up a wagon belonging to the Guard, and as some soldiers discussed whether the

BELOW, LEFT **Fusiliers of the Guard:** *Fusilier-Chasseur* **(left) and** *Fusilier-Grenadier* **(right); the latter wears the long trousers commonly used on campaign, with shako-ornaments removed. (Lithograph by Villain)**

BELOW, RIGHT **Junior members of the Grenadier corps, a** *Fusilier-Grenadier* **(left) and a** *Tirailleur-Grenadier* **(right), illustrating the different styles of lapels – square-cut for ordinary infantry and the point-ended light infantry pattern. (Print by Lacoste after Demoraine)**

draft animals were asses or mules, one remarked, "Don't you know that in the guard asses have the rank of mules?" This was evidence of the jealousy which existed on the part of the line towards the Guard's favoured status. As Blaze admitted, however, despite the complainings, everyone tried to attain it themselves: "In France, when everyone talked of equality, each was willing enough to share it with those who were above him, but not with those beneath him." On occasion this resentment even caused the men to come to blows.

French army pay varied not only according to rank, but according to unit or grade and length of service. It was highest among those receiving Guard rates. A Guard sergeant, for example, received 2 francs 22 centimes daily; his line equivalent was paid 62 centimes. Not all pay was actually received by the soldier, since, as in other armies of the period, the French had a system of deductions. Barrès recalled that of his daily pay of 23 sous 1 centime (a sou being five centimes), nine went to the mess for food, four for clothing and the remaining ten were paid every ten days as pocket money. Other deductions were also made (not always with complete financial probity in Barrès' opinion). Conversely there were rewards, bonuses and pensions (which were some 50 per cent higher than those of the line). Some of these furthered Napoleon's wish to make the members of the Guard indebted to him; others were necessary to assist men promoted from the ranks who had no private income. For example, when Parquin joined the Guard *Chasseurs à Cheval*, he received a grant of 3,000 francs to defray the cost of his new uniform. With financial grants for distinguished service and income from decorations like the *Légion d'Honneur* and the Order of the Iron Crown, it was possible for even ordinary soldiers to become fairly affluent. Take the chasseur whose horse was killed at Leipzig: rather than leave his troop to get another mount from the depot, he immediately bought a new horse from an officer, remarking that it was advisable to keep a year's money in hand for just such an eventuality.

The principal French decoration, the *Légion d'Honneur*, was instituted by Napoleon as a deliberate move to boost morale. It became the most coveted symbol of bravery or devotion to duty. Its award was accompanied by a pension, rising from 250 francs annually for an ordinary member to 1,000 francs for an *officier* and 5,000 for a *grand-officier*. Equally important was the honour which came with it. When Coignet received his cross, he was astonished to find that sentries were ordered to present arms to it and that cafés entertained holders of the decoration gratis; and when travelling on leave he told gendarmes that "the cross" was all the passport he needed. So greatly was the decoration prized that soldiers would often ask Napoleon for it in person.

The close relationship with Napoleon was another factor which distinguished the Guard. He created it as his personal fiefdom, and involved himself in every aspect of its administration and personnel. He would listen to the problems of the ordinary Guardsmen like a subaltern with his platoon, and the men would speak as freely to him as to their own officer. Napoleon knew hundreds of them not only by appearance but by name, and although his well known memory for names and faces might at times have been 'staged' to enhance his reputation, his memory does seem to have been phenomenal. For example, when a sergeant approached him to ask why he still hadn't received the *Légion d'Honneur*,

RIGHT *Voltigeur* of the Imperial Guard. (Lithograph after Villain)

RIGHT, BELOW *Gardes Nationales* of the Imperial Guard. (Lithograph after Villain)

BELOW *Conscrit-Grenadier* of the Guard; the shako is like that of the *Fusilier-Grenadiers* and the lapels are square-cut in Grenadier fashion, but in dark blue. (Lithograph after Villain)

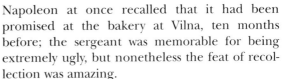

Napoleon at once recalled that it had been promised at the bakery at Vilna, ten months before; the sergeant was memorable for being extremely ugly, but nonetheless the feat of recollection was amazing.

The ease with which some Guardsmen spoke to their emperor reflected the almost familial atmosphere which existed between Napoleon and his Guard. He once reprimanded a chasseur of his escort for clumsiness after the man's horse had fallen; then Napoleon himself fell and the chasseur, having remounted, declared in a voice loud enough to be heard all around, that he was not the only clumsy person there. Such a rapport between emperor and troops emphasised the unique nature of their relationship and helps explain the absolute devotion he received from his Guardsmen. Perhaps indicative of the mutual trust is Coignet's account of how, when he was an ordinary soldier on duty at St. Cloud, he was entrusted to carry the King of Rome (Napoleon's baby son) while the child pulled the plume off his bearskin cap; it was one of the highlights of the Guardsman's life.

Relationships between officers and men were also more familiar than in some other armies. This was partly because many were drawn from the same social background: many officers, even those of the most exalted position, had begun their service in the ranks. Apart from the expected familiarity in the field, when officers and men were enduring the same tribulations, it was not even unknown for officers to socialise and entertain favoured 'other ranks' at home.

The Old Guard was distinguished by its appearance; unlike the remainder of the army, the *Grenadiers* and *Chasseurs à Pied* retained the old style long-tailed coat with lapels cut open to reveal the waistcoat, even after the introduction of the short-tailed, closed-fronted *habit-veste* for the Young Guard. Similarly, they retained the old-fashioned queue and hair-powder, and gold ear-rings were also virtually part of the uniform. They did use trousers on campaign at times, but they also retained the breeches and long gaiters which Blaze remarked were only suited to the mature veterans of the Guard with well developed legs, the gaiters hanging badly on the thinner legs of the young conscripts of the line. The use by the Guard of breeches and white cotton stockings in undress caused Coignet some embarrassment. When promoted to sergeant and permitted to carry a cane in undress and wear silk stockings, to conceal the shapelessness of his legs he bought a pair of false calves, concealing them by wearing two pairs of ordinary stockings with the silk ones on top. When entertained by a society lady who had taken a fancy to him, he found such difficulty in hiding the false calves (under the pillow) and in putting them on unseen in the morning that he never wore them again.

Prestige in the Guard was such that at home nothing less than a perfect appearance was tolerated: Guardsmen were inspected before leaving barracks and only allowed out if their appearance was immaculate. Coignet remarked that they were wonderfully smart but terribly uncomfortable. Such was the concern for the Guard's appearance that its first commander, Jean Lannes (later Marshal), exceeded his budget by some 300,000 francs. Napoleon ordered that he make good the sum within eight days or face court martial. Lannes had to borrow the money from Augereau and relinquished the position as commander of the Guard.

Conversely, at first discipline was somewhat lax (Guardsmen would attend morning roll-call in their shirt and breeches, without stockings, and then go back to bed.) That changed completely when Jean-Baptiste Bessières took over the Guard and reformed the administration, and the immaculate and brave Jean-Marie-Pierre-François Lepaige, comte Dorsenne, was appointed to the *Grenadiers à Pied*. 'Le beau Dorsenne', who rose to the rank of *Général de Division* and colonel of the grenadiers (and died in 1812 after an operation to treat an old wound), raised standards so thoroughly that the Guard became a model for the rest of the army. His Sunday inspections of the barrack rooms were meticulous: a speck of dust on the shelf where the bread-ration was kept resulted in four days in the guard room for the section's corporal. Dorsenne even lifted up the men's waistcoats to check upon the cleanliness of the shirt underneath. As a result, discipline (at least in the senior Guard regiments) was unmatched. With higher morale and a composition of veterans, the Old Guard's record of discipline was excellent, but desertion did afflict the more junior regiments; some of those apprehended were court martialled and others were treated as line deserters, being sent to a correctional depot for reassignment. Expulsion from the Guard and a return to the line was a great disgrace, as well as a loss of pay and privileges.

Flanqueur-Grenadier of the Imperial Guard. The single shoulder-belt is the one used by the rank and file of the Young Guard after the withdrawal of the *sabre-briquet* from all except NCOs and drummers. (Lithograph after Villain)

For the Guard, life at home and in barracks was very much better than for the line regiments. Napoleon took care to supervise the Guard's well-being in person. When inspecting a barrack room, he noticed that a tall grenadier had his feet hanging over the end of the bed; so Napoleon ordered that longer beds be provided for the entire Guard. Barracks were clean, well ventilated and tidy (though not without graffiti on the walls, according to contemporary pictures), but sometimes overcrowded. Barrès recalled that when the *vélites* were incorporated into the Old Guard units, they had to fit into beds which already had two occupants each. Light for the barrack rooms was provided by the men, who had to buy their own candles.

When not on campaign, the Guard's rations were much superior to those of the line. Even their method of eating was different: in general, French army practice was for each mess of between five and eight men to eat from a large

Veteran of the Imperial Guard.
(Print by Colin after Raffet)

communal bowl, but in the Guard each man had his own mess tin, so the purchase of a soup bowl was an almost symbolic first task for each new member of the Guard. In barracks the Guard hired female cooks, instead of each member of a mess taking his turn, as in the line. This was, in Blaze's words, "a Sybarite luxury" which was jeered at but nevertheless envied (an analogy to the inhabitants of Sybaris, a Greek city in ancient Italy, who were renowned for their luxurious lifestyle). Other employees were permitted in the Guard: cavalry NCOs and trumpeters, as well as officers, were allowed civilian grooms. Food was supposedly of a high standard. On one occasion Napoleon noticed bread of inferior quality, and declared that as he paid for white bread he would have it issued every day. Even on campaign, some three weeks before Friedland, he discovered sub-standard bread and remarked that it was not good enough for 'gentlemen'. This was thought to be a sarcastic remark in response to a complaint, until proper white bread was delivered the next day. (Criticisms were not uncommon, but then the Old Guardsmen were nicknamed *grognards* – 'grumblers' – and as one old NCO remarked to Blaze, they could be given roasted angels and they would still complain!) Even the horses of the Guard received favoured treatment; their daily allocation of forage was 6.5kg of hay, 5kg of straw and 8.5 litres of oats.

ON CAMPAIGN

The experience of campaign was varied for different parts of the Guard. Until its expansion by the formation of the Young Guard, it was an élite which usually accompanied Napoleon in person, the ultimate reserve, committed to action only in the most desperate of circumstances. Napoleon's attitude was exemplified by his unwillingness to commit the Old Guard to action at Borodino, even when the battle (conceivably the entire campaign) was in the balance; when pressed to bring the Guard into action, Napoleon demurred, conscious of his position in a hostile land, far from support, remarking, "And if there should be another battle tomorrow, where is my army?" This did nothing to increase the Guard's popularity with the rest of the army, and led to such ironic nicknames as 'Immortals' (bestowed upon the *Gendarmerie d'Elite*). This was also a source of frustration within the Guard, since it denied them the chance of distinction.

When the Guard *was* sent into action, it was likely to be in desperate situations, as at Marengo, where the Consular Guard won its first laurels in helping to hold the French right wing until the arrival of reinforcements saved the day. Less than 1,000 strong, they advanced with precision, the band playing and the men singing *'On va leur percer le flanc'*. They were described as "a redoubt built of granite", and so heroic was their conduct that Austrian officers who asked of prisoners the number of the men in the large bearskin caps, believed it when they were told 4,000. At Eylau, following the near-destruction of Augereau's corps, a Russian column came close to splitting the French centre and over-running Napoleon's own command-post. As usual, the Guard had been held in reserve, though not out of danger in this most sanguinary of battles. All morning they had remained immobile while under artillery fire. To meet the Russian attack, Dorsenne brought up two battalions (2nd Grenadiers and 2nd Chasseurs) with fixed bayonets, charging instead of prolonging the action by a lengthy exchange of musketry. Before they had arrived, Napoleon's own escort had had to charge the head of the Russian column to buy time. A successful repulse of the Russians, however, stabilised the French position.

Another critical deployment of the Guard occurred in 1809, at Aspern-Essling, when Napoleon was striving to hold a bridgehead over the Danube. He was greatly outnumbered and reinforcement was almost impossible because of damage to the bridges over the river. Here the Guard fielded two infantry divisions: the 1st Young Guard (*Fusiliers-Grenadiers* and *Chasseurs*, and *Tirailleurs-Grenadiers* and *Chasseurs*, a total of eight battalions); and the 2nd Old Guard under Dorsenne (two battalions each of *Grenadiers* and *Chasseurs à Pied*). This was the baptism of fire for the junior regiments, which went into action on the flanks of Napoleon's position as they attempted to hold the villages of Aspern and Essling. In Aspern the effort was eventually unavailing, and at Essling a counter-attack by four battalions, led by General Georges Mouton, proved insufficient to hold the position. General Jean Rapp was sent with two further battalions to extricate Mouton, but together Mouton and Rapp decided to mount another counter-attack and secured the position.

Napoleon actually commended Rapp for his disobedience, declaring that the safety of the army depended upon holding Essling. The Old Guard was deployed to help hold the centre, and they endured fierce bombardment as they closed towards the centre to fill the gaps blown by Austrian artillery fire as it smashed into the ranks

with such force that bearskin caps were flung as much as twenty feet into the air.

Dorsenne's courage at this juncture was an example to his men and epitomised the behaviour of the Old Guard: both his horses were killed, so he remained at the head of his men on foot, and when blown off his feet by the explosion of a shell, he called to his men, "Your general is not hurt. You may depend upon him, he will know how to die at his post!" (Such was his composure under fire that he would turn his back upon the enemy and face his own men, the better to reassure them, a form of cold courage which impressed all who witnessed it.)

Even under heavy bombardment the Old Guard disregarded its own plight to call to Napoleon to remove himself from the firing-line, threatening to lay down their arms unless he moved to a safer position. So severe were the losses at Aspern-Essling that some Guardsmen were sent to replenish the gun-crews, but they too were shot down and the artillery carriages shattered like firewood. Despite the casualties,

23

Sapeur du Génie of the Guard, wearing the distinctive helmet of the Old Guard element. (Print by Martinet)

however, the iron determination of the Guard helped secure the position until an orderly withdrawal was possible.

For the 1812 campaign against Russia, the Guard infantry was increased to three divisions: the 1st comprised the 4th-6th *Tirailleurs* and 1st, 5th and 6th *Voltigeurs*; the 2nd comprised the *Fusiliers-Grenadiers*, *Fusiliers-Chasseurs*, 1st *Tirailleurs*, 1st *Voltigeurs* and *Flanqueurs*; and the 3rd, the 1st to 3rd Grenadiers and 1st and 2nd *Chasseurs à Pied*. They were virtually destroyed in Russia, but the Guard was re-formed for subsequent campaigns; its enlargement changing its nature: from being originally a veteran élite (as the Old Guard was still regarded), by October 1813 it represented about one-third of the field army (almost 49,000 strong), rising to a nominal strength in 1814 of over 102,000.

Recruiting became increasingly difficult for the junior regiments, with raw conscripts filling the ranks and experienced men acting as cadres. Retired veterans and even invalids were recalled as NCOs.

The nature of some of the new soldiers is exemplified by the investigation carried out by the surgeon Baron Larrey into 48 young soldiers sentenced to death for deliberately injuring their hands to obtain their discharge. Among them were men from the Guard. After examination, Larrey proved them all innocent by having received their injuries through lack of training; by advancing with hands raised in front of their faces, and when in line of having been shot accidentally by the men behind!

Despite insupportable losses and the drafting in of ever more conscripts, the presence of the Guard was of immense importance in the last campaigns; as Napoleon remarked, in the defence of France they did more than could ever have been expected from mortal men.

Most of the Guard regiments were disbanded after the Bourbon restoration; some were kept as a separate category of troops – neither as part of the new Royal Guard nor of the line. Together with the Guardsmen who accompanied Napoleon to Elba and with the re-created Young Guard regiments, they served in the Hundred Days campaign. Even their efforts at Waterloo were unavailing, and the Guard was disbanded after the second restoration.

The role of the Guard cavalry was somewhat different. Fewer in number than the infantry, they were often kept as a reserve, brigaded together instead of being absorbed in the ordinary cavalry corps. Their imperial escort duty (see below) was of considerable significance, and they also took part in more conventional cavalry actions. Notable exploits include the charge of the Polish *Chevau-Légers* at Somosierra and the Guard cavalry's part in some of the great charges of the era, such as Eylau (**see text to Plate D**) and Waterloo.

In addition to employment as a cavalry reserve, the Guard performed all types of cavalry service. Charles Parquin, who in 1814 commanded a troop of Young Guard *Chasseurs à Cheval* (whose NCOs were all Old Guardsmen in the usual way), recalled a reconnaissance mission in which a squadron of 100 Guardsmen was assembled from his own *chasseurs*, dragoons, lancers and Mamelukes; when they fell upon an Allied encampment in a night attack, the enemy believed themselves to have been attacked by a brigade, because of the mixed uniforms of the attackers.

One of the great attributes of Napoleon's army – and especially of the Guard – was its ability to march: rapid forced marches over considerable distances were of major strategic importance. Marshal Ney attributed their ability to out-march their opponents to the 'sobriety and physical constitution' of the French soldier, and Blaze remarked that much could have been achieved had units been formed exclusively of men who could march for two days and two nights without rest. In an emergency, marches might be pressed at speed until the troops were on the point of collapse, with bands playing and drums beating to keep the men awake as they staggered onward. Such trials led to the quip that Napoleon made war not with arms but with his men's legs!

Sometimes the Guard were conveyed by carriage. For reasons of security, to frustrate the enemy's intelligence-gathering, Napoleon usually only left Paris when a campaign was about to commence, having first positioned most of his army. Since at least part of the Guard would generally accompany him, knowledge of the Guard's whereabouts could point to Napoleon's own location. (Wellington's memorandum of late April 1815, which noted the likelihood of French attack, began: "Having received reports that the Imperial Guard had moved form Paris upon Beauvais..." and proceeded to detail how his own army should be put in a state of readiness.) Elements of the Guard who had been retained until the last moment had to be hurried forward to join the men at the same pace as Napoleon's carriage. To prevent the total exhaustion which this

Engineers (*Sapeurs du Génie*) of the Guard (shown on the left), and an engineer in siege armour, including heavy cuirass and helmet (right) in full dress. (Print by Lacoste after H. Bellagé)

would have caused the men had they travelled on foot, they went by cart, with changes of horses and food prepared at various stages along the route. Travel by wagon was not, however, always preferable to marching: men were squashed into carts with their muskets, knapsacks and equipment – often ten or 12 men to each cart, without seats and sometimes even without straw on the floor. Barrès wrote that the experience of a 72-hour journey in 1806 "nearly broke our bones". Members of the Guard travelling from Spain to Germany for the 1809 campaign were conveyed partly by cabs requisitioned from Paris, with four men in each. They completed the next stage in heavy carts, 12 men to each vehicle, and were jolted miserably. They were then transferred to light carriages, and the earlier rapid rate of progress was restored. Apart from the discomfort of the vehicles, the Guardsmen experienced some embarrassment during their stop at Metz, where a large crowd had assembled to see them. As they changed their linen in the open air, such a wind was blowing that their shirts were lifted into the air and all the ladies in the crowd screamed at the sight!

Sometimes the men were permitted to put their knapsacks onto the regimental baggage vehicles, though in 1805 at least they were charged 20 centimes a day for the privilege.

Among the campaign baggage were the bearskin caps (nicknamed 'beehives') which distinguished the *Grenadiers* and *Chasseurs à Pied*. Initially they were used only in action, to make the Guard look as intimidating as possible (bicorn hats were worn at other times). In 1805 the bearskin caps were carried on the knapsack, in cardboard cases. The latter were reduced to pulp when exposed to rain, so the caps had then to be carried by hand. Later ticken bags, tied to the knapsack, were used instead.

The bicorn hat was normally worn 'athwart' (*en bataille*), but as a concession to the dreadful winter of 1806/7, Guardsmen on campaign in Poland were permitted to wear their hats 'fore-and-aft' (*en colonne*), which enabled them to fit fur ear-flaps, tied under the chin, in an effort to prevent frostbite. (This was a period of intense privation, but with the spirit which characterised the Guard, Barrès remarked philosophically that they were young, and used to it!) The burden of carrying two forms of head-dress on campaign was relieved when the Guardsmen were ordered to don their fur caps before Friedland (a sure sign that action was imminent), whereupon they spontaneously threw away their hats. Those bicorns were replaced, but a similar event occurred when the Guard was being hurried forward to Aspern-Essling: so rapidly was the Guard needed that they did not even have time to stop and put on their bearskin caps. Instead they put them on as they marched along, each man unpacking the cap of the man in front so as not to break step for even a moment. Again they took the opportunity to throw away their undress headgear, tossing their bicorn hats into the Danube as they passed.

Napoleon on campaign, wearing the uniform of the *Chasseurs à Cheval* of the Guard and protected by sentries from the *Grenadiers à Pied*. (Print after Meissonier)

The Emperor and his Guard: Napoleon reviews the *Grenadiers à Pied*. (Print after Raffet)

As well as regulation equipment, on campaign it was quite usual for the Guard to accumulate other belongings through various means. Orders were sometimes given against looting – in 1805 a chasseur *vélite* received the unusual punishment of having to hang the dead goose he had stolen around his neck until it became putrid – but in an army where foraging was a deliberate tactic to liberate it from the restriction of total reliance upon supply trains, looting was accepted. Sergeant Bourgogne of the Fusiliers provides a good example of the types of things the Guard might accumulate. His souvenirs from the abandoned city of Moscow in 1812 included a few practical belongings to protect him from the Russian winter: in addition to his regulation uniform and equipment, he carried a velvet-lined riding-cloak, a quilted silk waistcoat, an ermine-lined cape, a bearskin poncho, which fitted with the bear's head on his chest, a haversack on a silver cord (containing assorted loot including a silver and gold crucifix, a powder flask and a Chinese vase), and his knapsack, which contained several pounds of sugar, rice and a biscuit, half a bottle of liqueur, several gold and silver ornaments (including two silver pictures and assorted jewellery), a spittoon set with brilliants, a lump of silver gilt from the cross of Ivan the Great, and a gold and silver embroidered Chinese silk dress intended as a gift for any lady who might catch his eye.

A *chasseur* of the Guard acts as escort for an officer of Napoleon's staff on a reconnaissance mission. (Print after Meissonier)

Unpleasant though campaigning might be, the Guard did receive some concessions which caused some resentment among the remainder of the army. For example, if there were a high road, the Guard would march upon it while the others might have to struggle over open country; and the Guard generally received first pick of whatever supplies were available. This practice could have serious consequences, as seen on the retreat from Moscow, where the leading elements of the *Grande Armée* (including the Guard) consumed the contents of the supply depots at which they arrived, leaving little for the mass of the army which followed. This would seem to confirm Blaze's remark that either rations were in abundance or there was a famine. With the former there was frequently waste, since "the soldier gives himself no concern about the morrow: neither does it occur to him that in the following days other regiments will arrive at the position which he is about quitting, and that, while taking for himself what is necessary, it would be well to leave something for those who are to come after him. Such an idea never enters his head".

Despite any favoured treatment, on campaign the Guard was often just as short of rations as the rest of the army, especially when the enemy was so close that foraging or proper distribution of what supplies were

On campaign: a sentry of the *Grenadiers à Pied*, wearing the loose trousers commonly used on active service. (Print after Horace Vernet)

'Coquin de temps!'; *Grenadiers à Pied* of the Guard on the march in foul weather. (Print after Horace Vernet)

available became impossible. On the day before the battle of Jena, for example, all that Barrès could procure through foraging was a 5lb lump of sugar. That was all he had to eat on the day of the battle.

The situation was even worse during the dreadful winter of 1806/7, when food was in such short supply that even Napoleon had to request a potato from each of the Guard's messes to feed himself and his staff. He described his own sufferings in a letter to his brother Joseph, who had been complaining about campaigning in Italy. The privations endured by the Guard may be imagined when even Napoleon had to write: "I myself have been a fortnight without taking off my boots, in the middle of the snow and mud, without bread, wine or brandy, living on potatoes and meat, making long marches and counter-marches without any sort of comfort, fighting with our bayonets frequently under grapeshot; the wounded obliged to be removed on sledges, in the open air, to a distance of fifty leagues. To compare us with the army of Naples, making war in that beautiful country, where they have bread, wine, oil, linen, sheets to their beds, society, and even women, looks like an attempt at a joke… The army of Naples has no cause for murmuring. Say to them… 'your Emperor has been living for weeks upon potatoes, and bivouacking in the snows of Poland'…"

Although the French soldier was skilled in his ability to make himself comfortable even on campaign (the huts they built during the Peninsular War were much admired), the rapid movement which characterised Napoleon's system of warfare often gave no opportunity for such luxuries. With tents generally restricted to headquarters, bivouacs were usually made in the open field. This was not unpleasant in warm weather but demanded a strong constitution in the cold or wet. When near the enemy, although no restriction was normally placed upon the lighting of camp-fires, the soldiers generally slept without loosening their clothing or even removing their equipment, in case of an alarm during the night. Comfort might be gained from a camp-fire, though it was stated that lying close to it caused one side to roast, the other to freeze, and in extreme cold some believed it healthier not to subject the body to such extremes of temperature. Others suffered with eyes inflamed by camp-fire smoke. When further from the enemy, it was

possible to be more comfortable. The usual practice was to lie on bundles of straw or grass, sometimes with tree boughs as overhead shelter and sacks as sleeping-bags. The morning brought its own troubles, however, as Blaze recalled: "The moment for rousing at the bivouac is never amusing. You have slept because you were fatigued; but when you rise, your limbs feel stiff; your moustaches like tufts of clover, are impearled, every hair of them, with dewdrops; the teeth are clenched, and you must rub the gums for a considerable time to restore circulation... When it is rainy or cold, the situation is a great deal worse, and hence it is that heroes have the gout and the rheumatism."

Despite the Guard's privileged status, death and injury caused by the weapons of the period were just as terrible for them as for the troops of the line. Even if the Old Guard were held in reserve, bombardment at medium range, without being able to strike back, was considered worse than engaging at the forefront of a battle. In such situations the Guard's morale was crucial, and some of the heroism was scarcely human. One sergeant, whose leg had been carried off by a roundshot at Eylau, hopped away to the medical post, using two muskets as crutches, joking that with one leg his three pairs of boots would last him twice as long!

When it came to the care of the sick and wounded, the Guard enjoyed a distinct advantage over the line troops, partly because of their status and partly because their medical care was supervised by

TOP **A rest on campaign: soldiers (including a dragoon, right) take advantage of a convenient pile of hay, a typical scene observed by Albrecht Adam during the Russian campaign of 1812. (Print after Adam)**

ABOVE **A halt along the line of march: members of Napoleon's army depicted asleep during the invasion of Russia in 1812. (Print after Albrecht Adam)**

Dominique Jean Larrey himself, the greatest surgeon and humanitarian of the age. Initially the Guard had its own hospital near Paris, at Gros-Caillou, with a staff of experts and the very best of conditions. Other hospitals were used as the Guard increased in number.

Under normal circumstances, only a minority of battle casualties were killed outright; more fatalities were the result of a lack of rapid treatment and the onset of infection. With very little organised casualty-evacuation, wounded men usually had to make their way to the field hospitals established at the rear of the army. Many whose wounds might not have been fatal died from loss of blood or exposure, and those unable to walk might have to wait many hours, even days, before receiving treatment.

Amputation was a common solution for injuries to the limbs, both to save the time of hard-pressed surgeons and to reduce the patient's shock by completing the treatment as quickly as possible, given that anaesthetics were unknown. Hygiene too was neglected, which caused infection. At almost every level of the army medical service, from field surgeon to hospital, resources were usually inadequate to deal with the number of casualties caused by a major battle. The special treatment accorded the Guard demonstrates what might have been achieved with a larger and more general medical service.

As well as its own medical establishment, the Guard had a system of casualty-evacuation (designed by Larrey), and his staff had the right to appropriate any civilian billet for use as a hospital. They had absolute authority to take first pick of the available buildings – even before generals or headquarters staff. Statistics from the 1809 Danube campaign highlight the benefit of such relatively good standards of care.

On campaign: visiting a bivouac of the *Grenadiers à Pied*, Napoleon is offered a potato by one of his veterans. (Print after Raffet)

Of some 1,200 wounded Guardsmen, victims of Aspern-Essling and Wagram, by August half had been returned to their units, 250 were convalescencing back home, and only 45 had died. This recovery rate was unimaginable by the ordinary medical standards of the time.

Imperial Escort duty

Although on campaign the infantry of the Old Guard was usually in close attendance at imperial headquarters, the duty of protecting the emperor's person – the most important responsibility in the entire army – usually fell to the *Chasseurs à Cheval* of the Guard. On campaign Napoleon maintained a detachment of Guard cavalry under his personal command. They were drawn from the various regiments, of up to four squadrons strong. For immediate use he had the 'service squadron', a duty rotated among the Guard cavalry that ensured that no one squadron exhausted its horses in following Napoleon's long and rapid rides.

The closest escort of all was sometimes styled the *picquet*, and was usually drawn from the *Chasseurs à Cheval*, a small detachment constantly in attendance. It usually comprised a lieutenant in command, a sergeant, two corporals, 22 troopers and a trumpeter. The officer followed Napoleon's every movement and latterly only Berthier and Murat had precedence over him. A corporal and four troopers always rode ahead of Napoleon, and whenever he stopped to dismount or leave his carriage they did likewise, fixing bayonets when on foot and forming a loose, protective 'square' around him. Another of the troopers carried Napoleon's folio of maps and writing instruments.

When Napoleon estab-

BELOW **A bivouac on campaign: a self-portrait by the artist Albrecht Adam, who portrayed many scenes of the Russian campaign of 1812. The simple straw hut is typical of the temporary shelters which could be erected. (Print after Adam)**

BOTTOM **On campaign: cavalry bivouac around the large headquarters tents (visible in the background), a scene observed by Albrecht Adam during the Russian campaign of 1812. (Print after Adam)**

lished his headquarters in a house for the night, the officer of the escort occupied the next room to him, and the remainder of the detachment stood outside the building, horses saddled, ready for immediate action. Napoleon's own mount was kept there as well, supervised by two grooms. The escort was changed every two hours throughout the night, ensuring that it remained fresh. This duty was regarded as the most responsible in the army, and those who performed it thought it a prestigious honour. All were devoted to Napoleon and were rewarded appropriately by the bestowal of decorations and pensions.

The value of the escort was proven in 1812, on the day after the action at Maloyaroslavets. While reconnoitring, Napoleon was surprised by a party of Cossacks which burst from the cover of a wood, half-concealed by thick fog. The *picquet* and the small personal staff which accompanied Napoleon held them off until the 'service squadron' (on this occasion *Grenadiers à Cheval*) came up and drove off the enemy. An incident in this action exemplified the confusion which could occur in such circumstances: an officer named Le Couteulx, serving as ADC to Berthier, brandished a lance taken from a Cossack whom he had killed. Probably because his cloak concealed his distinctive French uniform, from waving of the lance, Le Couteulx was mistaken for a Cossack himself and was run through the body by a grenadier who believed him to be making for the emperor. Luckily the wound was not fatal: Le Couteulx survived the retreat and was conveyed home in one of Napoleon's own carriages.

Camp followers

An aspect of campaigning which seems unusual by modern standards was the presence of soldiers' families, who often accompanied the army – wives and children (legal or otherwise) of officers and men, as well as women who enjoyed a degree of official status as *cantinières* or *vivandières*, who sold food and drink to the soldiers, fulfilled an important function in the provision of rations, and were known to behave with great heroism. They accompanied their regiments into battle to dispense spirits from the small barrels they carried on a shoulder-belt. Such service was not without danger. Indeed, one of the Guard's 'characters' was Marie Tête-du-bois, *cantinière* of the 1st Grenadiers, who was married to a drummer killed at Montmirail. She had borne the drummer a son, who died in the defence of Paris, and was herself killed by a roundshot at Waterloo. Her mourning regiment

Napoleon on campaign, studying his maps amid a bivouac of the *Grenadiers à Pied*, who watch over him as he works. (Print after Raffet)

Inspection

A

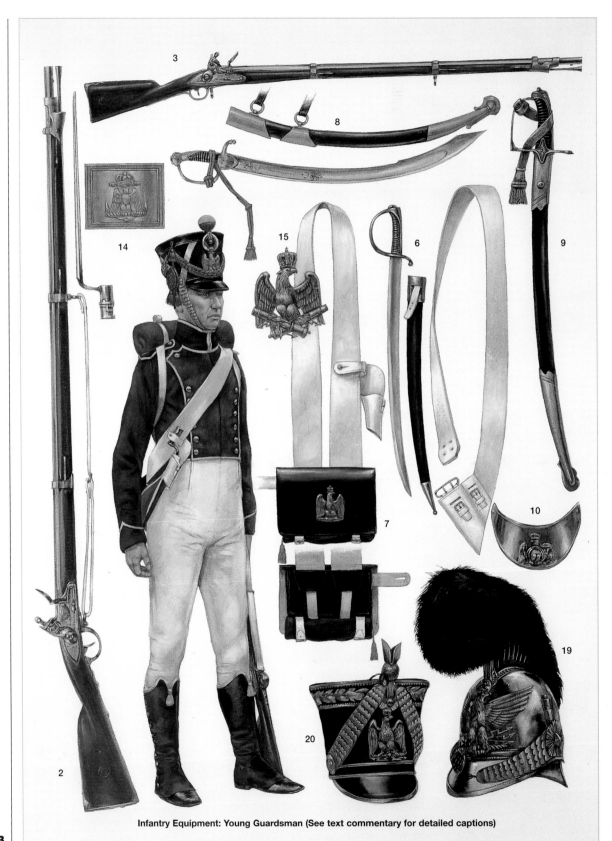

Infantry Equipment: Young Guardsman (See text commentary for detailed captions)

B

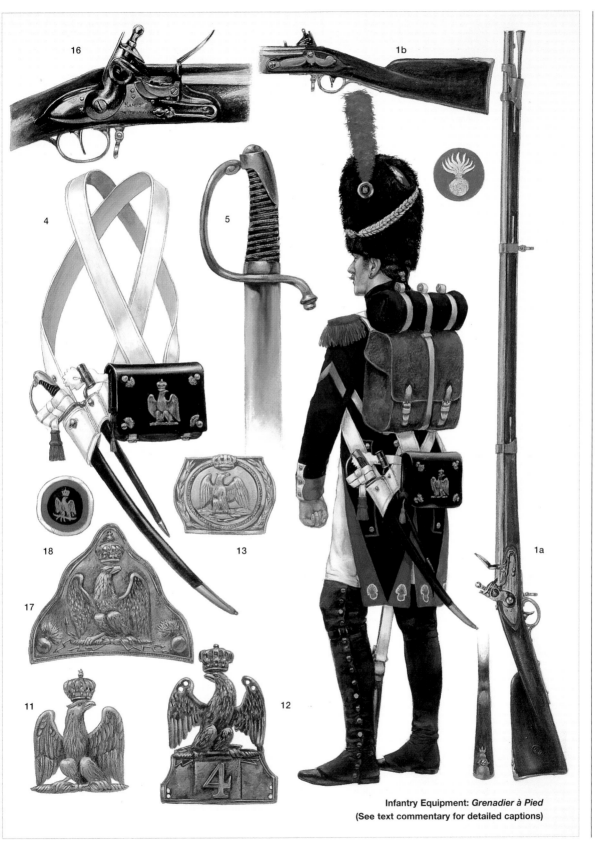

Infantry Equipment: *Grenadier à Pied*
(See text commentary for detailed captions)

C

Grenadiers à Cheval at Eylau, 8 February 1807

D

Imperial Escort Duty

E

F

Young Guard Infantry

Bivouac

Cavalry Equipment: *Chasseur à Cheval* (See text commentary for detailed captions)

H

Cavalry Equipment: Trooper, 1st (Polish) Lancers
(see text commentary for detailed captions)

Guard Artillery

J

The Retreat from Moscow

K

Casualties

A cavalry bivouac during the Russian campaign of 1812. This print after Albrecht Adam depicts dragoons of the Italian Royal Guard, but the scene is typical for the entire period, showing a hastily erected straw shelter.

erected a hasty marker which described her as 'dead upon the field of honour' and exhorted passers-by to salute her.

The plight of other women and children in times of trial, most notably during the retreat from Moscow, was awful to contemplate, and casualties among them were many. Some of the most heart-rending accounts written of this campaign concern the trials of such helpless non-combatants.

Many others accompanied the army to supply provisions as a commercial enterprise, or were just caught up in the immense throng of moving troops.

ARMS AND EQUIPMENT

Infantry

The equipment carried by the Guard infantry was similar to that used by the line troops, though it had some distinctive features. Among the most important items were the whitened leather shoulder belts (which for the Old Guard had distinctive stitched edges) supporting the cartridge box on the rear of the right hip, a frog for both sabre and bayonet at the left side, and a leather tag (for the Old Guard cut in the shape of a grenade) attaching the left edge of the cartridge box to the sword belt, to hold the belts in place. The cartridge box contained a wooden block which held two packets of 15 cartridges each and in the centre six drilled holes to hold indi-

Grenadiers à Pied drive off enemy cavalry. (Print after Horace Vernet)

vidual cartridges. It had a pocket for the tools needed to service the musket and for spare flints, including a wooden 'flint' for practice. (Elzéar Blaze recalled how those at the Fontainbleau school removed the interior of the cartridge box and filled it instead with pies baked specifically to fit!). The blackened leather flap of the cartridge box was used to display metal insignia, a crowned eagle for the Young Guard, a similar device for the *Chasseurs à Pied* (initially a horn), and for *Grenadiers* a crowned eagle with small grenades at the four corners of the flap (a large grenade until 1804). The folded forage-cap (*bonnet de police*) was carried beneath the cartridge box, held by two leather straps, and on campaign a protective fabric cover (which might be painted with the regimental device) could be fitted over the flap.

The knapsack was made of hide tanned with the hair on, carried on the back by straps over the shoulders, and ultimately with straps on the top in which a rolled greatcoat could be carried; when these were first added each man had to provide his own manner of fixing, so at first there was little uniformity. The knapsack carried all the soldier's possessions, and an equipment list of 1811 notes a larger pattern for the Guard than that carried by the line. Equipment carried on campaign might include a haversack, a canteen (acquired by the individual and of no regulated pattern, usually a metal flask, gourd, barrel, or bottle in a wicker case), mess-tin (*gamelle*) and cooking pot (*marmite*).

The standard French infantry musket was the pattern of *An IX* ('Year 9': the date for September 1800-August 1801 according to the 'Revolutionary calendar' introduced in France in 1792 and used until 1805). It was a variant of the 1777-pattern musket. A muzzle-loading

Grenadiers fighting in line, a scene from the early part of the Peninsular War, when the Guard accompanied Napoleon during his personal involvement in the war in Spain. The man in the left foreground is biting off the end of a cartridge; behind him, a rear-rank man passes a loaded musket to a man in the firing-line. (Print after H. Bellangé)

Napoleon follows the Polish *Chevau-Légers* of the Guard into the position captured by their charge at Somosierra. In this print, after Hippolyte Bellangé, a common error has been made in depicting the cavalry with lances. The lance was not adopted until some months after the action.

BELOW **The action at Benevente on 29 December 1808, one of the Guard's less successful actions during the Peninsular War, when General Charles Lefebvre-Desnouëttes was captured by Levi Grisdale of the British 10th Hussars, an event evidently depicted in this painting by Denis Dighton. (The Royal Collection © Her Majesty The Queen)**

flintlock, it had an overall length of 152cm, a calibre of 1.75cm and weighed about 4.5kg. Its metal fittings were iron, save for a brass pan. Although used by the Guard in large numbers, the Old Guard had a distinctive variety. The Consular Guard pattern had a raised cheek-piece, a lock with a patent pan-cover and brass fittings, including a butt-plate with a grenade-shaped finial set onto the top of the butt, and a similar finial on the trigger-guard. From 1802 the cheek-piece and patent pan were discontinued, and later a reinforced ramrod-channel was developed.

There was also a shorter musket, with an overall length of 143cm, which was sometimes styled in the *vélite* pattern and had the same brass fittings as the Guard musket. It was also carried by the foot artillery, whose equipment was of infantry pattern. The standard bayonet had a triangular-sectioned blade and a socket fitting with a locking ring. It was 46.5cm long.

Initially all infantry carried the short, slightly curved sword styled a *sabre-briquet*. (The latter was originally a term of derision derived from the verb '*bricoler*', meaning to rake a fire or to potter about.) The

The *Grande Armée* crosses the Niemen, heralding the beginning of the Russian campaign of 1812; Napoleon observes from the heights on the left, with his headquarters and escort of *Chasseurs à Cheval* in attendance; *Grenadiers à Pied* are in the left foreground. (Print after F. de Myrbach)

A desperate incident in the Russian campaign of 1812: Napoleon's escort and staff engage a party of Cossacks on the day after the battle of Maloyaroslavets, an action in which Napoleon could have been killed or captured. (Print after J. V. Chelminski)

ordinary pattern had a brass hilt cast in one piece – including the ribbed grip and single knuckle bow. The Old Guard had their own distinctive pattern, rather more decorative, with a down-turning quillon and a black leather grip bound with brass wire. For both patterns the scabbard was made of blackened leather with brass chape and throat: the Guard pattern attached to the belt-frog by a brass stud on the throat, but the line pattern had a buckled strap and brass loop on the throat. A fabric sword knot was normally carried (lace for NCOs) , and a woollen 'cravat' could be fitted around the base of the blade to prevent the ingress of water into the scabbard. In April 1813 the sword was withdrawn from the Young Guard (though retained by NCOs and drummers), which led to the use of the line-pattern single-shoulder-belt, carried over the left shoulder and supporting both the cartridge box and the bayonet-frog.

Napoleon confers with his engineer staff at Leipzig; the helmet of the *Sapeurs du Génie* of the Old Guard is clearly in evidence. (Print by Molte, after Grenier)

Officers normally used a waist-belt with decorative plate, from which was suspended a sabre in a frog. Swords were often of very fine manufacture, with a gilded hilt with a single knuckle-bow and a finely made blade with blued and gilt decoration, which might include the legend *Garde Impériale*. For the foot artillery the sabre had a slightly curved blade, a gilded scabbard and a semi-basket hilt incorporating the Guard artillery device of a crowned eagle upon crossed cannon barrels.

Cavalry

As for the infantry, leatherwork for the Guard cavalry was generally whitened, with stitched edges for the Old Guard. Variations did exist, however, notably the yellow buff belts with white edges used by the *Gendarmerie d'Elite*. Commonly two belts were carried over the left shoulder, one on top of the other, fastened together by a brass stud at the front. The lower belt supported the pouch or cartridge box and the upper carried the spring-clip from which the carbine could be suspended. There were two principal types of waist-belt, a wide version and a narrow, hussar pattern. Both supported a bayonet-frog (for the rank and file armed with carbines), two slings for the sabre, and for the light cavalry (excluding lancers) additional slings for the sabretache. The latter existed in decorated versions for 'dress' and plain for campaign; the former was sometimes carried with a waterproof cover for active service. Officers' belts, slings and pouches were laced or decorated.

Most of the cavalryman's equipment was carried in the valise at the rear of the saddle, or under the shabraque (including pistol-holsters at the front), with the folded cloak carried on top of the valise. The main types of shabraque included the pointed-end hussar version used by the light cavalry and horse artillery, and the heavy cavalry type, which consisted of a rectangular ended cloth with separate holster caps. The harness of both light and heavy patterns of saddle often included metal fittings bearing regimental insignia; some use was also made by chasseurs and horse artillery of fleece shabraques. Extremely elaborate 'dress' versions existed for officers, even made of panther-skin, and oriental-style horse furniture was used by Mamelukes.

The standard French light cavalry sabre was the *An XI* pattern, which had a curved blade 87.9cm long and a brass hilt with a triple-bar guard, down-turning quillon, large langets and a ribbed black leather grip with a brass oval set onto each side. The iron scabbard had two suspension rings. This was carried by some of the junior Guard cavalry, but the chasseurs (and from 1809 the lancers) of the Old Guard used a distinctive pattern, a curved-bladed sabre with a brass, single-bar stirrup hilt, large langets, straight quillon and ribbed black leather grip bound with brass wire. Its brass scabbard had an inset panel of black leather on each side. Officers of the *Chasseurs à Cheval* had a magnificently decorated version which included a lion-head pommel, langets bearing a classical mask, and an engraved, gilded scabbard bearing a crowned eagle badge affixed between the suspension rings.

Several patterns of sabre were carried by the heavy cavalry. The *Grenadiers á Cheval* originally used the old sabre of the *Garde du Directoire*, with its slightly curved blade and semi-basket hilt incorporating a large grenade device. They also used the *An IV* chasseur sabre, with a hilt incorporating three wide bars and a slightly curved blade. Later they had

RIGHT **Napoleon (who was trained as a gunner) aims a cannon of the Horse Artillery of the Guard at Montereau. Although the gunners wear hussar-style uniform, their officer has a *chasseur*-style coat with Guard aiguillette. The gunner second from right carries a portfire, and a reserve, with smouldering match, is stuck in the ground to the right of the gun, to re-light the gunner's portfire if it should go out. The ammunition-chest, which was transported upon the gun-trail, has been positioned on the limber (extreme left) for easy access. (Print after E. Lami)**

A unit of recent conscript calls to Napoleon that he may trust them as much as the Grenadiers of the Old Guard in the background. (Print after Raffet)

a straight bladed sabre of *An IX* pattern, with a brass semi-basket hilt incorporating a grenade within a voided circle, and a leather scabbard with brass throat, suspension-ring locket and chape. This was itself succeeded by two sabres of a similar pattern, but with a very slightly curved blade of the style known as '*à la Montmorency*". It had a similar hilt and brass scabbards with black leather inserts. This final pattern (its variants were issued in 1802-03 and 1810) was also carried by the Guard Dragoons and by the *Gendarmerie d'Elite* from 1806-07. The latter had previously used the *An IX/XIII* heavy cavalry sabre with straight blade, brass four-bar semi-basket hilt with ribbed leather grip and iron scabbard. Officers carried sabres of superior manufacture, with additional decoration including elaborate hilts.

The principal cavalry carbine was the short-barrelled *An IX/XIII* pattern, which had a brass butt plate, trigger guard and forward barrel-band; on the reverse side of the stock to the lock was a brass plate to which was usually attached an iron rod, joined to the rearmost iron

BELOW *Grenadiers à Pied* of the Guard in 1814, wearing their typical campaign uniform, including long trousers, with cap-cords and plume removed; Napoleon is visible in the right background, using a *chasseur* of his escort as a rest for his telescope. (Print after A. Bligny)

barrel-band. Upon this rod was an iron ring which attached to the spring-clip on the shoulder belt. From 1802 the *Grenadiers à Cheval* carried a carbine measuring 111.3cm overall. It differed from the *An IX* model in that its wooden stock extended as near to the muzzle as for an infantry musket and it was equipped with three brass barrel-bands. From 1806 the *Grenadiers à Cheval* used the *vélite* musket.

The Guard Dragoons used the *An IX* dragoon musket, similar to the infantry pattern but with a barrel-length of 102.9cm. (141.5cm overall), with brass fittings save for an iron middle band and swivels

The standard cavalry pistol was the *An XIII* model, 35.2cm overall, with brass fittings including straps which extended down the butt and joined the butt-plate. Other weapons were also used: the Polish *Chevau-Légers*, for example, were at first equipped with captured Prussian sabres and firearms, then received French patterns, including the *An XI* sabre, which was replaced by the chasseur pattern in 1809. Hardly any use was made by the French army of rifled weapons, although rifled carbines for dragoons are mentioned.

The lance was used by Guard regiments designated as lancers, and by the *Eclaireurs* and Lithuanian Tartars. The

Injured *Grenadiers à Pied* of the Guard attempt to make their own way out of the firing-line to seek medical treatment. (Print after H. Bellangé)

With the medical services unable to provide rapid treatment for all the wounded, the injured were often left to their own devices: this grenadier has improvised a tourniquet from his musket-sling for his injured leg. (Print after Horace Vernet)

Polish regiment was armed with lances only from late 1809, hence their original designation *Chevau-Légers*. The lances had wooden shafts, and the original pattern had a flattened 'ball' below the blade which would help to prevent over-penetration, and the 1812-pattern without. A story to illustrate the pride the Guardsmen took in their weapons was recounted by Captain Cavalié Mercer, commander of 'G' Troop of the British Royal Horse Artillery at Waterloo. On the day after the battle he encountered a group of wounded Frenchmen, among whom was a Guard lancer named Clement. The latter sat amid his fellows, exhorting them not to exhibit want of fortitude in the presence of their enemies and bear their sufferings like men. The lancer had lost a hand, been hit by bullets in the body and had a broken leg – "his suffering, after a night of exposure so mangled, must have been great; yet he betrayed it not. His bearing was that of a Roman… I could not but feel the highest veneration for this brave man, and told him so, at the same time offering him the only consolation in my power – a drink of cold water, and assurances that the waggons would soon be sent round to collect the wounded. He thanked me with a grace peculiar to Frenchmen". Mercer's attention then turned to the man's lance, stuck upright in the ground beside him. He begged the weapon as a keepsake, whereupon "the old man's eyes kindled as I spoke, and he emphatically assured me that it would delight him to see it in the hands of a brave soldier, instead of being torn from him, as he feared, by those vile peasants". The lance had been his companion in many campaigns, and he was genuinely pleased that Mercer should want it, ensuring that it should not be dishonoured by the hands of a scavenger. Mercer's groom carried it through the rest of the campaign, and in 1827 it was used as a reference by the committee proposing to redesign the British Army's regulation weapon. Ever after, on Waterloo Day, Mercer stuck the lance in his lawn and decked it with roses and laurel as a tribute to a brave man who had carried it in battle and then entrusted it to a fellow soldier.

The Mamelukes carried distinctive weapons, including an oriental sabre with a long, curved blade and a curve-ended hilt with straight quillons. The scabbard was carried in oriental fashion on a cord over the shoulder. A dagger and a pair of pistols in a holster were tucked into the waist-sash, and another pair of pistols were kept in the saddle holsters. They also had a carbine or blunderbuss, and either a mace,

A common method of casualty-evacuation observed by Albrecht Adam during the Russian campaign of 1812: a wounded officer is carried from the battlefield seated upon a musket. (Print after Adam)

battle-axe or both. The pistols were of a distinctive pattern, with the butt swelling to a flattish base upon which was fixed a brass plate. (Apparently 503 of these were manufactured.) The blunderbuss (*tromblon*) was 79cm overall and had a bell-mouthed muzzle and fittings. Only 73 were produced.

Other units

The Seamen of the Guard used distinctive equipment. Their leatherwork was black and originally included a waist-belt and small pouch, with a short sabre (probably the naval *briquet*) carried on a shoulder belt. By about 1805 the waist belt seems to have been worn over the shoulder, producing cross-belts, and in 1806 two sets were issued, one varnished for full dress and the other waxed. The cartridge box supported by the belt over the left shoulder bore an anchor badge, which was changed to an eagle and anchor in 1805/6. Its belt had a brass anchor badge added after 1811. The belt over the right shoulder supported the sabre on slings and a bayonet frog; its brass rectangular buckle was replaced by a brass plate bearing an anchor in 1805/6, and by a plate bearing a crowned eagle and anchor in about 1811. In 1806 a distinctive sabre was introduced, with a broad, curved blade, a brass hilt with single knuckle-bow and down-turning quillon, large langets bearing an anchor, and a black leather grip bound with brass wire. The Otto MS shows a sabre with no knuckle-bow, similar to a recorded NCOs' sabre. Originally one-third of the corps was to be armed with sabres, one-third with axes and the remainder with pikes, but as the axes and pikes are not mentioned in inventories of September 1805, presumably they had been discontinued. The unit's musket was presumably the *An IX* naval pattern. Officers originally carried an épée upon a white leather waist-belt, but from May 1807 they were ordered to carry a sabre. Presumably the épée was then reserved for walking out and for evening wear – the belt changed to black leather with indented gold lace edging.

Troops of the train initially wore a white leather waist belt and a *sabre-briquet*, but early in 1810 it was replaced by the belt already worn by the line train. This could be worn on the waist or the shoulder. It was styled a *ceinturon-baudrier* ('waist-shoulder belt'), still with a frog for the *briquet*, and the belt plate bore an eagle over crossed cannon barrels. Drivers of horse batteries wore waist-belts with slings and light cavalry sabres.

There can have been few worse sights than the aftermath of a battle: this is an eye-witness representation of scenes around Borodino by the Württemberg officer Christian Faber du Faur. (Print after Faber du Faur)

Units are listed below in order of formation. Unless stated otherwise, all were disbanded after Napoleon's abdication in 1814, and those which remained in existence, or were re-formed upon Napoleon's return in 1815, were disbanded between September 1815 and the end of that year. In addition, some Guardsmen accompanied Napoleon to Elba as his bodyguard.

Grenadiers à Pied: 1st Regt. formed 1799; 2nd Regt. formed April 1806, incorporated in 1st in 1809, re-formed May 1811; both re-titled *Corps Royal des Grenadiers de France* May 1814, reverting to old name 1815. 3rd (Dutch) Regt. formed September 1810 as 2nd, renumbered 3rd in May 1811, disbanded February 1813; new 3rd (not Dutch) and 4th regts formed April 1815.

Chasseurs à Pied: 1st Regt. formed 1799, became chasseurs 1801; 2nd Regt. formed April 1806, incorporated in 1st in 1809, re-formed May 1811; both re-titled as *Corps Royal des Chasseurs à Pied de France* May 1814, reverting to old name 1815. 3rd and 4th regts formed April and May 1815 respectively.

Grenadiers à Cheval: formed December 1799, became *Grenadiers à Cheval* December 1800; re-titled as *Corps Royal des Cuirassiers de France* May 1814, reverting to old title 1815.

Chasseurs à Cheval: formed December 1799; re-titled *Corps Royal des Chasseurs à Cheval de France* May 1814, reverting to old title 1815.

Artillerie à Cheval: formed as *Artillerie Légère* December 1799, designated *Artillerie à Cheval* 1806, reorganised 1815.

Train d'Artillerie: formed September 1800, re-formed April 1815.

Veteran Company: formed July 1801; retained under the Bourbons.

Mamelukes: formed October 1801.

Gendarmerie d'Elite: formed March 1802, re-formed 1815.

Seamen (Marins): formed September 1803, re-formed 1815.

Vélites: *Grenadiers* and *Chasseurs à Pied* formed July 1804, *Grenadiers* and *Chasseurs à Cheval* September 1805, Artillery April 1806; merged with parent units.

Dragoons: formed April 1806, titled *Dragons de l'Impératrice* 1807, re-titled *Corps Royal des Dragons de France* 1814, reverting to old title 1815.

Ouvriers d'Administration: formed April 1806.

Gendarmes d'Ordonnance: formed September 1806, disbanded October 1807.

Fusiliers-Chasseurs: formed October 1806.

Fusiliers-Grenadiers: formed December 1806.

Lancers (Chevau-Légers-Lanciers): 1st (Polish) Regt. formed March 1807 as *Chevau-Légers*, became lancers 1809, squadron went to Elba; 2nd (Dutch) Regt. formed September 1810, re-titled *Corps Royal des Lanciers de France* May 1814, reverting to old title 1815; 3rd (Polish) Regt. formed July 1812, incorporated into 1st in March 1813.

Artillerie à Pied: formed April 1808, re-formed April 1815.

Tirailleurs-Grenadiers: 1st and 2nd regts formed January and April 1809 respectively; became 1st and 2nd *Tirailleurs* December 1810.

Tirailleurs-Chasseurs: 1st and 2nd regts formed March and April 1809 respectively; became 1st and 2nd *Voltigeurs* December 1810.

Napoleon's farewell to the Guard after his abdication, at Fontainebleau, on 20 April 1814. He declared to his guardsmen, "I cannot embrace you all, but I shall embrace your general." After General Petit, he kissed the 'Eagle' three times. (Print after Horace Vernet)

Conscrits-Grenadiers: 1st and 2nd regts formed March 1809; became 3rd and 4th *Tirailleurs* February 1811.

Conscrits-Chasseurs: 1st and 2nd regts formed March 1809; became 3rd and 4th *Voltigeurs* February 1811.

Italian Vélites: *Vélites* of Turin and Florence formed April 1809.

Gardes Nationales de la Garde: formed January 1810, became 7th *Voltigeurs* February 1813.

Engineers (Sapeurs du Génie): formed July 1810, re-formed April 1815.

Tirailleurs: 1st-4th regts formed as above from existing units; 5th and 6th formed May 1811; 3rd-6th *bis* regts formed January, disbanded March 1813; 7th formed January 1813; 8th, March 1813; 9th-13th, April 1813; 14th-19th, January 1814; 1st-6th regts re-formed April 1815.

Voltigeurs: 1st-4th and 7th regts formed as above from existing units; 5th formed May 1811; 6th, August 1811; 3rd-6th *bis* regts formed January, disbanded March 1813; 8th formed March 1813, 9th-13th, April 1813; 14th-19th, January 1814; 1st-6th regts re-formed April 1815; 7th and 8th, May 1815.

Pupilles: formed March 1811.

Train des Equipages: formed August 1811; re-formed April 1815.

Flanqueurs-Chasseurs: formed September 1811.

Veteran Artillery (Cannoniers-vétérans): formed January 1812.

Lithuanian Tartars: formed August 1812, incorporated in *Eclaireurs* 1813.

Flanqueurs-Grenadiers: formed March 1813.

Gardes d'Honneur: 1st-4th regts formed April 1813.

Eclaireurs: 1st (Grenadier), 2nd (Dragoon) and 3rd (Lancer) regts formed December 1813.

REFERENCES

Of the many works which in some way concern the Imperial Guard, the following will be found especially useful:

Bucquoy, Cmdt. E. L., *Les Uniformes du Premier Empire.* Series of books which re-print the Bucquoy uniform-cards – see next entry

Lt. Col. Bucquoy & G. Devautour (ed.), *La Garde Impériale: Troupes à Cheval* and *La Garde Impériale; Troupes à Pied* (both Paris 1977)

Elting, J. R., *Swords Around a Throne: Napoleon's Grande Armée* (London 1989). An invaluable modern study of the French Army, including the Guard

Lachouque, H., & Brown, A. S. K., *The Anatomy of Glory: Napoleon and his Guard* (London 1962)

Malibran, H., *Guide... des Uniformes de l'Armée Français* (Paris 1904; reprinted Krefeld 1972). Primarily concerned with uniform regulations but includes information on organisation and unit-lineage.

Rousselot, L., *L'Armée Française.* Series of uniform plates

Willing, P., *Napoléon et ses Soldats: L'Apogée de la Gloire* (Paris 1986). Includes illustrations of extant items of arms and equipment and portraits relating to the Guard

Details of uniforms and equipment may also be found in the Osprey *Men-at-Arms* series: *Napoleon's Guard Infantry I* (**MAA 153**) and *II* (**MAA 160**) and *Napoleon's Specialist Troops* (**MAA 199**)

Memoirs and biographies relating to the Imperial Guard which are available in English include the following:

Barrès, J. B. (ed.), trans. B. Miall, *Memoirs of a Napoleonic Officer* (London 1925)

Blaze, E. (ed. Lt. Gen. Sir Charles Napier), *Lights and Shades of Military Life* (London 1850); originally published as *La Vie Militaire sous le Premier Empire, ou Moeurs de garnison, du bivouac et de la caserne* (Paris 1837); a reprint of the 1850 edition is titled *Life in Napoleon's Army: The Memoirs of Captain Elzéar Blaze* (London 1995) and a new

There was some ill feeling between Napoleon's most faithful followers and those who embraced with enthusiasm the restoration of the Bourbon monarchy in 1814. If not completely convincing in all aspects of uniform detail, this painting by Denis Dighton represents the disdain of an officer of the ex-Imperial Guard (left) when confronted by two National Guardsmen sporting the white Bourbon cockade. (The Royal Collection (c) Her Majesty The Queen)

translation by Col. J. R. Elting is titled *Military Life under Napoleon; The Memoirs of Captain Elzéar Blaze* (1995)

Bourgogne, A. F. B. F. (trans. & ed. P. Cottin & M. Henault), *The Memoirs of Sergeant Bourgone* (London 1899); reprinted with introduction by D. G. Chandler (London 1979)

Chlapowski, D. (trans. T. Simmons), *Memoirs of a Polish Lancer: the Pamietniki of Dezydery Chlapowski* (Chicago 1992)

Coignet, J. R. (with introduction by Hon. Sir John Fortescue), *The Note-Books of Captain Coignet, Soldier of the Empire* (London 1929)

Parquin, C. (trans. & ed. B. T. Jones), *Charles Parquin: Napoleon's Army* (London 1969)

Richardson, R.G., *Larrey: Surgeon to Napoleon's Imperial Guard* (London 1974)

Periodicals: much information may be found in French journals such as *Carnet de la Sabretache*, *Uniformes* and *Tradition*.

French cavalry, evidently intended to represent the red-uniformed 2nd (Dutch) *Chevau-Légers-Lanciers* of the Guard, engaged in furious combat with Highlanders (who from their blue facings must represent the 42nd) during the Waterloo campaign; a painting by Jan A. Langendyk. (The Royal Collection © Her Majesty The Queen)

THE PLATES

Napoleon salutes, and in return is cheered by, a battalion of the *Grenadiers à Pied* at Waterloo. (Print after Ernest Crofts)

A: INSPECTION

This scene of an officer inspecting a detachment of Guardsmen in front of a barracks represents the principal formations which made up the Guard in the uniforms of about 1812: the corps of *Grenadiers* and *Chasseurs à Pied*, seamen, artillery and cavalry. **1** The sergeant (his rank is indicated by gold and red cap-cords, epaulettes and sword knot, and gold rank-bars on the lower sleeve) represents the *Grenadier à Pied*. Long-service chevrons were worn on the left upper sleeve – one for ten years' service, two for 15-20 years and three for 20-25 years. **2** The officer, also from the Grenadier corps, wears the shako of the Fusiliers. **3** The *Chasseur à Pied* wears the distinctive plate-less cap and a coat of light infantry style, with pointed lapels and cuffs. **4** The seaman wears the braided dolman used in full dress. **5** The gunner of the Guard Horse Artillery wears that corps' hussar-style full dress (an alternative was a chasseur-style coat and braided waistcoat), and the cavalryman (**6**) is a trooper of the Empress' Dragoons. The aiguillette was a mark of Guard status used by cavalry, artillery and staff, but was never worn with hussar-style uniform.

B AND C: INFANTRY EQUIPMENT

The *Grenadier à Pied* (right) shows how the ordinary equipment was worn, excluding the undress hat in ticken cover carried on the knapsack in the earlier part of the period. The Young Guardsman (left) wears the distinctive green uniform of the *Flanqueurs*, with the distinctions of the *Flanqueurs-Grenadiers* in the white chevrons on the sides of the shako, red cords and red and yellow pompon. He has the line-pattern single shoulder-belt used by the rank and file of the Young Guard after the withdrawal of the *sabre-briquet*. The cartridge box and bayonet were carried on the same belt. The detail illustrations show: (**1a** and **1b**) Guard-pattern musket with distinctive brass fittings; (**2**) *An IX* musket as carried by the Young Guard; (**3**) *Vélite*-pattern shorter musket; (**4**) cartridge box and belts with the insignia of the *Grenadiers à Pied*; (**5**) Guard-pattern sabre; (**6**) line-pattern *briquet* and shoulder belt as used by the Young Guard; (**7**) Young Guard shoulder-belt with bayonet frog attached; (**8**) seaman's sabre; (**9**) officer's sabre; (**10**) officer's gorget, bearing the usual crowned eagle device combined with the horn insignia of the *Chasseurs*; (**11**) design of Young Guard shako-and cartridge box plate; (**12**) shako-plate bearing regimental number, attributed to the Young Guard; (**13**) officer's belt plate; (**14**) officer's belt-plate bearing the insignia of the seamen; (**15**) artillery insignia as used on shako and cartridge box; (**16**) musket lock; (**17**) bearskin cap plate, *Grenadiers à Pied*; (**18**) bearskin cap cockade; (**19**) helmet of the *Sapeurs du Génie* of the Old Guard; (**20**) officer's shako, *Voltigeurs*, with the foliate upper band favoured by the chasseur corps (stars by grenadiers).

Waterloo: surrounded by his *Grenadiers à Pied* of the Guard, **Napoleon surveys the battlefield. The wounded officer (head bandaged, left foreground) has picked up a musket from one of the casualties. (Print after Raffet)**

D: GRENADIERS À CHEVAL AT EYLAU, 8 FEBRUARY 1807

The Guard cavalry served with distinction in many actions, but few were in such severe conditions as at Eylau, when it participated in the massed French charges executed in freezing weather and blinding snowstorms. They saved Napoleon from defeat after the infantry of his centre had been shattered. Instead of the cavalry being used in the usual manner, in delivering the final blow to break an enemy already wavering, they had to charge to prevent the Russian army from breaking Napoleon's line. Although Bessières led the Guard cavalry, the actions of General Louis Lepic are perhaps best known. He almost missed the battle due to an attack of rheumatism in the knees, but Larrey's treatment got him sufficiently mobile to lead his command. Early in the battle, when the Guard had to sit immobile under Russian fire, Lepic shouted to those of his men who were ducking to avoid the shot: "Heads up, by God! Those are bullets, not turds!" (This translation follows Lachouque, H., & Brown, A. S. K., *The Anatomy of Glory*, London 1962, p.88; this episode formed the subject of the memorable painting by Edouard Détaille titled from the French-language version of the exhortation, *'Haut les têtes! La mitraille n'est pas de la merde!'*, exhibited at the Salon of 1893.)

The illustration here depicts a later stage of the battle, when Lepic led his grenadiers in the charge. Once through the Russian line, the French cavalry rallied in its rear and charged back through it. As the survivors reassembled in the French position, Lepic was missing; he arrived soon after with a small party which had followed him through the Russian lines, declined a call to surrender, and cut its way free. Napoleon greeted his return by remarking that he feared Lepic had been captured; no, replied Lepic, Napoleon might receive a report of his death, but never of his surrender!

The grenadiers shown here follow the Otto MS in depicting the single-breasted *surtout,* evidently worn on campaign in place of the white-lapelled dress coat, though the bearskin caps are shown with the cords and plume which might have been donned before action. The men wear queues and are clean-shaven, though the Otto MS shows short hair and moustaches. The trumpeter rides a black horse instead of the expected grey and has a black cap; despite later illustrations, white fur caps may not have been worn by trumpeters.

E: IMPERIAL ESCORT DUTY

This plate depicts members of the '*picquet*' of *Chasseurs à Cheval,* which provided the closest escort for Napoleon and his immediate staff, as they might have appeared in the 1809 campaign. Four chasseurs with carbines at the ready formed a 'square' around the Emperor, dismounting when he dismounted. The remainder, including the *picquet*'s officer and the trooper carrying the portfolio of maps, remained close at hand. In the Austerlitz campaign the chasseurs apparently wore their pelisses, in 1806/7 their *surtouts* and in 1809 their dolmans. Sometimes the chasseurs wore overalls on campaign and a cloak and cape in bad weather, but for Napoleon's personal escort, the shoulder cape alone was worn, without the cloak, so that his position might be identified by the dress of his escort. Napoleon may be seen in the background in his traditional campaign dress of a greatcoat over the undress coat of the *Chasseurs à Cheval*. He is attended by a marshal and an *officier d'ordonnance*, one of his senior aides, wearing the distinctive light blue uniform with silver lace introduced in early 1809.

F: YOUNG GUARD INFANTRY

This plate depicts *Tirailleurs* of the Young Guard in action: *Tirailleurs-Grenadiers* with red shoulder straps, *Tirailleurs-Chasseurs* with green shoulder straps, and green shako-pompons. Both corps served in Curial's 1st (Young Guard) Division in the desperate fighting at Aspern-Essling. It is recorded that not until August 1809 did NCOs of the Young Guard wear the epaulettes of the Guard; sergeants and above were otherwise distinguished by gold and red shako cords and lace, and sword knots. In April 1813 the *Tirailleurs* were ordered to wear the 1812 *habit-veste* with lapels closed to the waist. Shako cords and lace were abolished, and the *sabre-briquet* was restricted to NCOs and drummers, with other ranks adopting the line-pattern shoulder-belt supporting both cartridge-box and bayonet. The officer here wears the uniform of the *Fusiliers-Grenadiers*. Various stages in the process of loading the musket are also illustrated – first biting off the end of the cart ridge (the ingress of gunpowder into the mouth was partially responsible for the raging thirst which afflicted men in combat), pouring enough of the powder to fill the priming pan on the lock, then inserting the remainder, with the lead ball, into the muzzle and ramming it home. Three or four shots per minute was the usual rate of fire, which slowed if the musket became fouled with burned powder or the barrel became so hot that it became impossible to use. It is recorded that in such circumstances, with water usually in such short supply, it might be necessary to urinate upon the musket to cool the metal enabling the user to continue firing.

G: BIVOUAC

On campaign, Napoleon's headquarters, including his own large tent, was generally guarded and surrounded by a battalion of the Old Guard. The relationship between emperor and his devoted and trusted followers was such that he could speak familiarly and joke with them without compromising the respect, even adoration, which they felt for him. This plate depicts Napoleon visiting a bivouac of the *Grenadiers à Pied*, where their evening camp fires would boil their soup or stew. When the enemy was near, the men would remain ready for immediate action, not even removing all their equipment or their coats.

The grenadiers are depicted in their campaign dress of long trousers and caps devoid of plume and cords. As a sign of his close connection with the Guard, Napoleon generally wore the undress coat of the *Chasseurs à Cheval*, which became as familiar a sight as his grey greatcoat and plain hat worn 'athwart'. It was remarked that this uniform did not display him to the best advantage, at least in later years. Sir Henry Bunbury, who met him in July 1815, described him as "fat, and his belly projects; but this is rendered more apparent by the make of his coat, which has very short lappels [sic] turned back, and it is hooked tight over the breast to the pit of the stomach, and is there cut away suddenly, leaving a great display of white waistcoat".

The last act of the Imperial Guard: at the close of the battle of Waterloo a square of the Old Guard (centre) attempts to cover the withdrawal of the French army. (Print after Raffet)

H AND I: CAVALRY EQUIPMENT

These plates depict cavalry equipment. The trooper of the *Chasseurs à Cheval* wears the alternative to the hussar-style uniform, the long-tailed coat with aiguillette and braided waistcoat. The trooper of the 1st (Polish) Lancers also wears the Guard aiguillette. He carries the original pattern of lance with a flattened 'ball' below the blade; the sabre is the Guard light cavalry type as carried by the *Chasseurs à Cheval*. The detail illustrations show: (**1**) sabre, belt and sabretache of the *Chasseurs à Cheval* (several variations of the sabretache existed; the one shown here had an embroidered face with a brass eagle affixed); (**2**) *Grenadiers à Cheval* sabre of the last pattern, as carried also by dragoons and *Gendarmerie d'Elite*; (**3**) *An XI* light cavalry sabre; (**4**) *An XI/XIII* cavalry carbine; (**5**) *An XIII* pistol; (**6**) cavalry belt with slings and bayonet-scabbard, with the plate used by the *Grenadiers à Cheval* – note the leather loop which held the bayonet-socket in position; (**7**) cavalry shoulder-belts, showing pouch and carbine clip; (**8**) heavy cavalry pattern horse furniture with separate holster caps – this is the pattern used by the *Grenadiers à Cheval* before the grenade badges were replaced by an imperial crown in 1809; (**9**) light cavalry horse furniture – the pattern used by the Horse Artillery; (**10**) Horse Artillery sabretache of the type used from 1810 – prior to that date the design was embroidered, with a large crown over an eagle, over large cannon barrels, with a spray of oak and laurel at the sides; (**11**) officer's belt plate, *Grenadiers à Cheval*; (**12**) dragoon's pouch badge; (**13**) officer's shako plate, 2nd *Gardes d'Honneur*.

J: GUARD ARTILLERY

This gun-team of the Old Guard wears campaign uniform with the peaked fur bonnet adopted in May 1810, with cords and plume removed for active service (when the scarlet rear patch, bearing a yellow grenade, could be concealed by a cover). Before 1810 the Guard Foot Artillery wore shakos (which were worn by the Young Guard companies throughout). The Old Guardsmen wore queues and belts with stitched edges. They are shown with trousers tucked into short gaiters instead of the long gaiters, and blue breeches worn on more formal occasions.

The officer wears a single-breasted *surtout*, a coat often worn on campaign. A typical gun crew, as depicted here, consisted of eight men (one a 'spare' to replace any injured man). One man held the double-ended rammer and 'sponge', the former for ramming the projectile and propellant down the gun-barrel, the latter covered with fleece, to be dipped in water after every shot to extinguish any sparks which might have remained in the barrel and which could cause premature ignition of the next round. This gunner was assisted by the 'loader', who stood at the other side of the gun-barrel. A senior gunner or NCO aimed the gun by moving the handspikes which slotted into the rear of the trail; elevation was by the screw beneath the cascabel or closed end of the barrel. Rounds were contained in an ammunition chest which rode upon the gun-trail and was removed to a safe distance in action. The rounds were conveyed to the loaders at the muzzle in a satchel carried by another gunner. As the charge was inserted in the barrel, another gunner, sometimes called the 'ventsman', leaned over the barrel and put his finger over the touch-hole to prevent the ingress of air from igniting any smouldering powder which might remain in the barrel; he wore a protective leather finger-stall. After the charge was rammed home, it was pierced by another gunner, by a spike through the touch-hole (this gunner wore a waist-belt and pouch which carried the spike and fuse which was then inserted into the touch-hole). Finally, with all the gunners standing clear of the recoil, a seventh gunner ignited the charge with a portfire, a rod carrying a length of smouldering slow-match. After the gun fired, it was re-positioned after the recoil and the sequence repeated. Casualties among gun-crews could be severe, and at times of crisis infantrymen could be deployed to make up the numbers, perhaps most famously at Wagram, where Napoleon called for 20 men from each Old Guard company to fill the gaps in the gun-crews. Another celebrated incident involved Grenadier Brabant at Marengo, who despite a shattered hand loaded and fired an abandoned four-pounder to cover the withdrawal of his comrades until he became too weak from loss of blood to serve it any longer.

K: THE RETREAT FROM MOSCOW

The Guard can have endured nothing so terrible as the retreat from Moscow in 1812. The Russian campaign of that year virtually destroyed that (large) part of the Guard which participated in the campaign, though by virtue of its discipline the Guard did not collapse into the mass of fugitives in the same way as other parts of the *Grande Armée*. The nature of the ordeal may be gauged from statistics concerning the three Grenadier and two *Chasseur à Pied* regiments. On 10 October they mustered some 195 officers and 6,005 men; on Christmas Day, at the end of the retreat, there were present 159 officers and 1,312 men; by February 1813, with the sick and injured deducted, the Old Guard numbered only 415 chasseurs and 408 grenadiers. The Young Guard fared no better: by early December 1812 the entire force under arms mustered only 800 men.

This plate depicts part of the Guard infantry trudging through the snow on this most terrible of marches. It is based in part upon contemporary records such as those of the Württemberg officer C. G. Faber du Faur, whose eye-witness pictures convey the horror of the struggle both against the elements and the pursuing Russian forces. Members of the Old Guard and Fusiliers are shown wearing their greatcoats (onto which the epaulettes were affixed) and campaign trousers; among variations recorded by Albrecht Adam in his illustrations are waterproof covers for the fur cap and trousers tucked into gaiters. Officers might wear bicorn hats and cloaks or capes. In addition to the regulation clothing and equipment, all manner of civilian and other items were pressed into service to protect against the cold, including furs, scarves, cloaks or lengths of fabric serving as cloaks, and even strips of fur wrapped around the head to protect the ears from frostbite. Although the plight of the soldiers must have been appalling, that of the camp-followers and soldiers' and officers' wives and children can scarcely be imagined.

L: CASUALTIES

This scene shows the evacuation of a casualty from the battle-front. Despite the enhanced system of medical care maintained by the Guard, with its own ambulances, the removal of casualties was still somewhat haphazard, with

many of the wounded having to make their own way, or be helped, to the nearest medical attention. Here, an officer of the *Fusiliers-Chasseurs* is carried by one of his men, aided by a driver of the Guard artillery train whose caisson can be seen in the background. The wounded man is sitting upon a musket held horizontally between the two bearers, a common method of carrying casualties. The scene is as might have appeared in Russia in 1812: the *Fusilier-Chasseur* private wears his campaign overalls and has removed the plume and cords from his shako; the driver wears the 'iron grey' jacket with pointed lapels, braided waistcoat and breeches, and shako-ornaments, which apparently were worn in the Russian campaign. The wounded man is greeted by Baron Larrey, wearing the uniform depicted by Lejeune in

Waterloo: the last stand of the Old Guard, with General Pierre Jacques Etienne Cambronne (1770-1842) shouting defiance in the centre. According to tradition, when called upon to surrender he cried, "The Guard dies but does not surrender!" He denied saying this and instead probably uttered an expletive which became known as '*le mot de Cambronne*'. He was wounded and captured in the last stage of the battle by Hew Halkett who commanded the 3rd Hanoverian Brigade of Wellington's 2nd Division. (Print after Georges Scott)

his painting of Borodino. The dark blue coat with crimson facings has the gold aiguillette indicative of Guard status.

Notes sur les planches en couleur

A Le sergent représente le Grenadier à Pied. 2 officier, qui appartient lui aussi aux Grenadiers, porte le shako des Fusiliers. 3 Le Chasseur à Pied porte le calot sans plaque, bien reconnaissable, et une capote dans le style d'infanterie légère, avec des revers de col et de manchettes pontus. 4 Le marin porte le dolman orné de passementeries utilisé avec uniforme de parade. 5 Le canonnier de Artillerie Montée des Gardes porte uniforme de parade de ce corps, dans le style hussard, et le soldat de cavalerie (6) fait partie des Dragons de Impératrice.

B et C Le Grenadier à Pied (à droite) illustre la manière de porter le matériel ordinaire, le Jeune Garde (à gauche) porte uniforme vert bien particulier des Flanqueurs, avec les distnctions des Flanqueurs-Grenadiers, qui sont des chevrons blancs sur les côtés du shako, des galons rouges et un pompon rouge et jaune. La boîte à cartouches et la baionnette étaient portées sur la même ceinture. Les illustrations détaillées montrent: (**1a et 1b**) Mousquet de Gardes, avec garnitures spéciales en cuivre; (**2**) un mousquet IX utilisé par la Jeune Garde; (**3**) Mousquet plus court, de modèle Vélite; (**4**) boîte à cartouches et ceintures portant les insignes des Grenadiers à Pied; (**5**) Sabre de Gardes; (**6**) briquet line-pattern et bandoulières utilisés par la Jeune Garde; (**7**) Bandoulière de Jeune Garde, avec porte-baionnette; (**8**) sabre de marin; (**9**) sabre officier; (**10**) hausse-col officier, qui porte aigle couronné habituel, combiné avec insigne des Chasseurs, en forme de corne; (**11**) moddle de plaque de shako et cartouchière des Jeunes Gardes; (**12**) plaque de shako, qui porte le numéro du régiment, attribuée à la Jeune Garde; (**13**) plaque de ceinture officier; (**14**) plaque de ceinture officier qui porte les insignes des marins (**15**) insignes artillerie utilisées sur le shako et la cartouchière, (**16**) percuteur de mousquet; (**17**) plaque de bonnet à poil, Grenadiers à Pied; (**18**) cocarde de bonnet à poil; (**19**) casque des Sapeurs du Génie de la Vieille Garde; (**20**) shako officiers, Voltigeurs.

D La Garde montée servit avec distinction dans de nombreuses actions, mais rarement dans des conditions aussi difficiles qu'à Eylau, durant les charges françaises massives exécutées par grand froid et sous les tempêtes de neige aveuglantes. Les Grenadiers sauvèrent Napoléon de la défaite après la destruction de infanterie au centre. Cette illustration dépeint une scène plus tardive de la bataille, lorsque Lepic se trouvait à la tête des Grenadiers pour la charge.

E Cette planche décrit des membres du Apicquet des Chasseurs à Cheval, qui représentaient escorte la plus proche de Napoléon et de son état-major immédiat, tels qu'ils auraient pu être durant la campagne de 1809. Quatre chasseurs armés de carabines faisaient le vide et formaient un Accaré autour de Empereur et descendaient de cheval en même temps que lui.

F Cette planche représente des Tirailleurs de la Jeune Garde en action: Tirailleurs-Grenadiers avec des bandoulières rouges, Tirailleurs-Chasseurs avec des bandoulières vertes et un pompon de shako vert. Ces deux corps servirent dans la 1e Division de Curial (Jeune Garde) dans les combats acharnés Aspern-Essling. Cet officier porte uniforme des Fusiliers-Grenadiers.

G Durant les campagnes, le quartier-général de Napoléon, y compris sa propre tente, était généralement gardé et entouré par un bataillon de la Vieille Garde. Cette planche représente Napoléon visitant un bivouac des Grenadiers à Pied, alors que leur feu de camp servait à cuire leur soupe ou leur ragôut. Les grenadiers sont décrits en uniforme de campagne, composé un pantalon long et un calot sans panache et sans cordons.

H et I Ces planches décrivent le matériel de cavalerie. Le soldat infanterie des Chasseurs à Cheval porte un manteau à grands pans avec une aiguillette et un gilet orné de passementeries, qui pouvait remplacer uniforme de style hussard. Le soldat infanterie du 1er Lanciers (Polonais) porte également aiguillette des Gardes. Il porte une lance du modèle original, qui comporte une Aboule aplatie en dessous de la lame; le sabre est celui porté par la cavalerie légère des Gardes comme les Chasseurs à Cheval. Les illustrations détaillées montrent: (**1**) sabre, ceinture et sabretache des Chasseurs à Cheval (plusieurs variantes du sabretache existaient). Celle qui est illustrée ici portait une face brodée ornée d'une aigle en cuivre); (**2**) Sabre des Grenadiers à Cheval, un modèle plus tardif, porté également par les dragons et la Gendarmerie Elite; (**3**) Un sabre XI de cavalerie légère; (**4**) une carabine de cavalerie XI/XIII; (**5**) Un pistolet XIII; (**6**) une ceinture de cavalerie avec bretelle et fourreau à baionnette, avec la plaque utilisée par les Grenadiers à Cheval - notez la boucle de cuir qui tenait en place la douille de la baionnette; (**7**) bandoulières de cavalerie, avec sac et crochet à carabine; (**8**) sellerie de cavalerie lourde, avec fontes séparées; (**9**) Sellerie de cavalerie légère; (**10**) Sabretache Artillerie montée du type utilisé à partir de 1810, avec une grande couronne qui surmonte un aigle, le tout sur de grands canons, avec un brin de chêne et de laurier sur les côtés; (**11**) Plaque de ceinture officier, Grenadiers à Cheval; (**12**) plaque de giberne de dragon; (**13**) plaque de shako officier des 2e Gardes Honneur.

J Cette équipe de pièce de la Vieille Garde porte un uniforme de campagne avec le bonnet de fourrure à visière adopté en mai 1810, les cordons et le panache étant ôtés pour le service actif (durant lequel écusson arrière rouge, qui portait une grenade jaune, pouvait être caché par une housse). Avant 1810, la Garde Artillerie à pied portait le shako (qui était porté par les compagnies de Jeunes Gardes). Les membres de la Vieille Garde portaient une queue et une ceinture aux bords cousus. On les voit ici avec une culotte rentrée dans les guêtres courtes au lieu des guêtres longues et la culotte bleue portée pour les occasions plus officielles. Officier porte un surtout à boutonnage simple, souvent porté en campagne.

K La Garde n'a sans doute jamais connu quelque chose de plus terrible que la retraite de Moscou en 1812. Cette planche représente une partie de infanterie en train de progresser dans la neige durant cette marche terrible. On voit les membres de la Vieille Garde et des Fusiliers qui portent leur capote et leur pantalon de campagne. Parmi les variantes enregistrées par Albrecht Adam dans ses illustrations, citons les housses imperméables pour les bonnets à poil et le pantalon rentré dans les guêtres. Les officiers portaient parfois un bicorne et un manteau ou une cape.

L Cette scène représente évacuation un blessé du front. Ici, un officier des Fusiliers-Chasseurs est porté par un de ses hommes, aidé par un chauffeur du train artillerie de la Garde, dont on voit le caisson en arrière-plan. Le blessé set assis sur un mousquet à horizontale entre les deux porteurs, une méthode courant ede transport des blessés.

Farbtafeln

A1 Der Feldwebel repräsentiert den Grenadier à Pied. **2** Der Offizier, der ebenfalls dem Grenadier-Korps angehört, trägt den Tschako der Füsiliere. **3** Der Chasseur à Pied trägt die charakteristische Mütze ohne Plättchen und eine Jacke im Stil der leichten Infanterie mit spitz zulaufenden Revers und Manschetten. **4** Der Matrose trägt mit Tressen besetzten Dolman, wie er bei der Paradeuniform üblich war. **5** Der Schütze der berittenen Gardeartillerie trägt die Paradeuniform im Husarenstil dieses Korps, und der Kavallerist (**6**) ist ein Soldat der Dragoner der Kaiserin.

B und C Der Grenadier à Pied (rechts) demonstriert, wie die normale Ausrüstung getragen wurde, der Soldat der Jungen Garde (links) trägt die charakteristische grüne Uniform der Flanqueurs mit dem Erkennungszeichen der Flanqueurs-Grenadiers in den weißen Winkeln an den Seiten des Tschakos, roten Kordeln und einem rot-gelben Pompon. Die Patronentasche und das Bajonett waren am gleichen Gurt befestigt. Die Darstellungen im Detail zeigen folgendes: (**1a und 1b**) Muskete des Gardemodells mit den charakteristischen Messingbeschlägen; (**2**) Eine IX-Muskete, wie sie die Junge Garde hatte; (**3**) Kürzere Muskete des Vélite-Modells; (**4**) Patronentasche und Gürtel mit den Abzeichen der Grenadier à Pied; (**5**) Säbel des Gardemodells; (**6**) `BriquetA des Mannschaftsmodells und Schulterriemen, wie von der Jungen Garde benutzt; (**7**) Schulterriemen der Jungen Garde mit Bajonettschlaufe; (**8**) Matrosensäbel; (**9**) Offizierssäbel; (**10**) Offiziershalsberge mit dem üblichen Kaiseradlerabzeichen und dem Hornabzeichen der Chasseurs; (**11**) Muster des Plättchens auf dem Tschako und der Patronentasche der Jungen Garde; (**12**) Tschakoplättchen mit der Regimentsnummer der Jungen Garde; (**13**) Offizierskoppel; (**14**) Offizierskoppel mit den Abzeichen der Matrosen; (**15**) Artillerieabzeichen, das auf dem Tschako und der Patronentasche auftaucht; (**16**) Musketenschloß; (**17**) Plättchen auf der Bärenfellmütze, Grenadiers à Pied; (**18**) Kokarde der Bärenfellmütze; (**19**) Helm der Sapeurs du Génie der Alten Garde; (**20**) Offizierstschako, Voltigeurs.

D Die Gardekavallerie zeichnete sich in vielen Schlachten aus, doch wurden nur wenige unter solch schwierigen Bedingungen gefochten wie die Schlacht bei Eylau, wo sie an den massiven französischen Angriffen teilnahm, die bei kalten Temperaturen und bittern Schneestürmen stattfanden. Sie rettete Napoleon vor der Niederlage, nachdem die Infanterie der Mitte zerschlagen worden war. Die Abbildung zeigt eine spätere Phase der Schlacht, als Lepic seine Grenadiere zur Attacke führte.

E Diese Farbtafel zeigt Angehörige des `PicquetA des Chasseurs à Cheval, die als Leibwache für Napoleon und seine engsten Mitarbeiter fungierten, wie sie im Feldzug 1809 ausgesehen haben könnten. Vier Chasseurs mit geladenem Karabiner bildeten ein `ViereckA um den Kaiser und stiegen vom Pferd ab, wenn er abstieg.

F Diese Farbtafel zeigt die Tirailleurs der Jungen Garde in Aktion: Tirailleurs-Grenadiers mit roten Schulterriemen, Tirailleurs-Chasseurs mit grünen Schulterriemen und grünen Tschakopompons. Beide Korps dienten in Curials 1. (Junge Garde) Division im verzweifelten Kampf bei Aspern-Essling. Der Offizier trägt die Uniform der Fusiliers-Grenadiers.

G Auf Feldzügen wurde Napoleons Hauptquartier, einschließlich seines eigenen großen Zelts, allgemein bewacht und war von einem Bataillon der Alten Garde umgeben. Diese Farbtafel zeigt Napoleon beim Besuch eines Lagers der Grenadiers à Pied, wo man auf dem Lagerfeuer wahrscheinlich eine Suppe oder einen Eintopf kocht. Die Grenadiers sind in ihrem Feldanzug abgebildet, der aus langen Hosen und Mützen ohne Federbusch und Kordeln besteht.

H und I Auf diesen Farbtafeln ist die Kavallerieausrüstung abgebildet. Der Soldat der Chasseurs à Cheval trägt die Alternative zur Uniform im Husarenstil, nämlich die Jacke mit langem Schoß und Achselschnur und eine mit Tressen besetzte Weste. Der Soldat des 1. (polnischen) Lanzenträger trägt ebenfalls die Achselschnur der Garde. Er hat eine Lanze des ursprünglichen Modells bei sich, die unterhalb der Klinge eine flachgedrückte `KugelA aufweist; der Säbel entspricht dem Typ der leichten Kavallerie der Garde, wie ihn die Chasseurs à Cheval hatten. Die Darstellungen im Detail zeigen folgendes: (**1**) Säbel, Gürtel und Säbeltasche der Chasseurs à Cheval (die Säbeltasche gab es in unterschiedlichen Ausführungen; die hier abgebildete wies eine verzierte Vorderseite auf, die am Messingadler befestigt war); (**2**) Säbel ist dieser Modell, leicht dasselbe Modell der Grenadiers à Cheval, wie ihn auch die Dragoner und die Gendarmerie d'Elite hatten; (**3**) leichter Kavalleriesäbel der Serie XI; (**4**) Kavalleriekarabiner der Serie XI/XIII; (**5**) XIII-Pistole; (**6**) Kavalleriegürtel mit Schulterriemen und Bajonettscheide mit dem Plättchen, das die Grenadiers à Cheval verwendeten - man beachte die Lederschlaufe, an der die Bajonetthülle befestigt wurde; (**7**) Schulterriemen der Kavallerie mit Beutel und Karabinerladestreifen; (**8**) Pferdeausstattung der schweren Kavallerie mit separaten Halfterkappen; (**9**) Pferdeausstattung der leichten Kavallerie; (**10**) Säbeltasche der berittenen Artillerie der Machart, wie sie ab 1810 verwendet wurde - sie wies eine große Krone über einem Adler sowie einen Eichenlaub- und Lorbeerzweig an der Seite; (**11**) Offizierskoppel, Grenadiers à Cheval; (**12**) Beutel eines Dragoners; (**13**) Plättchen am Offizierstschako, 2. Gardes d'Honneur.

J Diese Schützenmannschaft der Alten Garde trägt die Felduniform mit der Pelzhaube mit Schirm, die im Mai 1810 eingeführt wurde. Bei aktivem Dienst wurden die Kordeln und der Federbusch entfernt (und das scharlachrote Rückteil, auf dem eine gelbe Granate aufgetragen war, konnte durch einen Überzug verdeckt werden). Vor 1810 trug die Garde-Artillerie zu Fuß Tschakos (die man bei den Kompanien der Jungen Gardeal tragen gesehen wurde). Die Angehörigen der Alten Garde trugen Zöpfe und Gürtel mit genähten Rändern. Sie sind in Hosen abgebildet, die in kurze Gamaschen anstatt in die langen gesteckt sind, und in blauen Breeches, die zu formellen Anlässen getragen wurden. Der Offizier trägt einen einreihigen Überzieher, ein Mantel, der im Feld häufig getragen wurde.

K Die Garde kann wohl nichts schlimmeres erlebt haben als den Rückzug von Moskau 1812. Diese Farbtafel zeigt einen Teil der Garde-Infanterie, wie sie sich auf dem schlimmsten aller Märsche durch den Schnee schleppt. Die Angehörigen der Alten Garde und Füsiliere sind in Mänteln und Feldhosen abgebildet. Albrecht Adam belegt in seinen Illustrationen unterschiedliche Variationen der Aufmachung, so etwa wasserdichte Bezüge für die Pelzmütze und in Gamaschen gesteckte Hosen. Die Offiziere trugen unter Umständen einen Zweispitz und Umhänge oder Capes.

L Diese Abbildung zeigt den Abtransport eines Verwundeten von der Schlachtlinie. Hier wird ein Offizier der Fusiliers-Chasseurs von einem seiner Männer getragen, dem ein Zugführer des Garde-Artilleriezuges behilflich ist, dessen Wagenkasten man im Hintergrund sieht. Es Verwundete sitzt auf einer Muskete, die zwischen den beiden Trägern waagerecht gehalten wird. Es war allgemein üblich, Verwundete so zu tragen.